NO
RED MEAT

BRENDA SHRIVER ✐ ANN TINSLEY

FISHER
BOOKS

**Library of Congress
Cataloging-in-Publication Data**

Shriver, Brenda J., 1941-
    No red meat cookbook.

    Includes index.
    1. Vegetarian cookery. 2. Low-fat diet—Recipes.
3. Low-cholesterol diet—Recipes. I. Tinsley, Ann.
II. Title.
RM236.S57 1989   641.5'63   89-11632
ISBN 1-55561-021-8

Publishers: Bill Fisher
               Helen Fisher
               Howard Fisher
               Tom Monroe, P.E.

Coordinator: Helen Fisher
Editor: Veronica Durie
Art Director: Josh Young
Drawings: David Fischer
Cover photo: DeGennaro Associates, Los Angeles

Published by Fisher Books
PO Box 38040
Tucson, AZ 85740-8040
(602) 292-9080

Copyright 1989 Fisher Books

Printed in U.S.A.
Printing 10 9 8 7 6 5 4 3 2

Contents

Dedication

To Our Family
My Greatest Blessing

Acknowledgments

A special thank you to Ann Tinsley, Ph.D., R.D., my co-author, for providing all the nutritional information in this book and for her support and faith.

I wish to thank the people who have shared their recipes with me. In addition, thanks to Sally Schaper, who furnished helpful editorial comment and suggestion, and my friends and family, who supported me with their love and prayers.

I am grateful to my family for their moral support, suggestions and patience over the years as I was developing these recipes. A special thanks to my son, John, III, for overwhelming patience in helping me with the complexities of our computer. I am also thankful to my daughter, Audrey, for her encouragement and suggestions in developing new recipes. And finally, I am most grateful to my husband, John, my most vocal critic and strongest supporter.

—**Brenda Shriver**

About the Authors

BRENDA J. SHRIVER grew up in a small town in Tennessee, where she assisted in a family-owned restaurant. After she moved to Ohio, she worked in different restaurants during summer vacations, learning various aspects of food preparation and handling. After marriage to her husband, John A. Shriver, Jr., she was delighted to have the time and freedom of her own kitchen to put into practice all she had been taught about cooking. Due to John's career with a major corporation, they have lived in several different areas of the country. In their travels they have learned to love different ethnic foods and Brenda has acquired many new recipes.

ANN M. TINSLEY, Ph.D., R.D., received her bachelor's degree from Penn State and served her dietitic internship at Brooke Army Hospital in San Antonio, Texas. She received her master's and Ph.D. degrees from the University of Arizona. Dr. Tinsley is an associate professor of Nutrition and Food Science at the University of Arizona. She works as a food and nutrition education consultant and has evaluated, tested and revised recipes for eight other cookbooks.

This Book Is For You!

This cookbook is for people with coronary heart disease (CHD) and for their families who are at high risk of developing the disease. It is also for the growing number of people who are choosing to eat more wisely to avoid future health problems.

Seven years ago we learned my husband John had coronary heart disease (CHD). John's cardiologist told him to change his eating habits and continue a vigorous exercise program.

I acquired several "heart cookbooks" and started a new way of cooking. After several disappointments, our family agreed most of the recipes were not very tasty and too strict or not strict enough. And we missed some of our family favorites. I began to experiment by preparing a new dish and letting the family sample it. If it got thumbs down, I tried the recipe again, making necessary changes until we agreed the food was tasty and worth repeating. I created my own recipes by adapting and converting old and new recipes. I've also created many original dishes.

People started asking for my recipes. I was always happy to share. But there was one major problem—all the new recipes were in my head! So it was back to the kitchen. This time I went with pen and paper, measuring, cooking and writing as I worked. I had more recipes than I realized. So at the urging of family and friends, I wrote this cookbook.

I want to share my recipe collection with other people. Over the years I've noticed friends and family members with CHD who have failed to stick to their medically restricted diet. At first I couldn't understand it, but after our experience I began to see the difficulty of following this type of diet.

There are kinds of "heart cookbooks"—the cookbook for a more sophisticated palate and very strict cookbooks. I talked to many people about "heart diets." They were enthusiastic about trying new recipes, especially the more sophisticated ones. Unfortunately, the novelty soon wore off. And after a few weeks of eating food made of unfamiliar ingredients, they gradually went back to their old eating habits. People who chose the stricter recipes soon became bored with food that had little taste and wasn't satisfying. They gradually returned to their old eating habits.

My recipes will satisfy most people who are interested in improving their diets. At the same time, these are familiar dishes like "Mom used to make."

In *No Red Meat,* I've included:
🐦 Vital nutritional information with each recipe.
🐦 Informational charts on cheese, fish and chicken.
🐦 List of herbs and spices, with suggested uses.
🐦 Menu suggestions.
🐦 Helpful hints precede each section.
🐦 A wide variety of recipes—
  Normal food for everyday,
  Special food for entertaining or special occasions.
  Traditional food for holidays.

In this collection, I have created healthy, low-fat, low-cholesterol recipes every family member can enjoy.

Some are simple enough for the beginning cook. Others are more complicated for the experienced cook who likes to spend more time in meal preparation. Many are my family's old favorites that I converted without sacrificing good taste.

These recipes were created specifically for my husband's diet. While his sodium intake is not restricted, I use very little salt in my cooking. I rely on herbs and spices. This is why I use canned products in some recipes and call for salt in others. If you are on a salt-restricted diet, make the substitutions I've suggested, but use your own ideas or use salt-free products.

My husband does not have a weight problem, so he is permitted some sugar. Our family is fond of desserts, so there is an extensive selection of desserts.

His diet limits the number of grams of fat per day he can consume. With this in mind, I give a lot of consideration to meal planning. If the entrée contains more fat than usual, I am careful with the remainder of the meal. I make sure other dishes are lower than usual in fat. The same is true for desserts. If the dessert has more fat than usual, I plan a fish or vegetarian entrée, keeping in mind total fat intake for the day.

Meal planning requires time and effort to maintain a healthy, satisfying diet, but it is possible. Once you become familiar with shopping and these recipes, it will become second nature.

It is my hope that by sharing my recipes with you, whether on medically restricted diets or just health conscious, you will realize food can be delicious and healthy.

—Brenda Shriver

Introduction to Low-Cholesterol Cooking

Excessive consumption of fats is a major national health problem. According to Dr. C. Everett Koop, U.S. Surgeon General, "If you are among the two out of three Americans who do not smoke or drink excessively, your choice of diet can influence your long-term health prospects more than any other action you might take."

Cardiovascular heart disease (CHD) is the leading cause of death in the United States. About 48% of all North Americans die of CHD or related diseases. The major risk factors associated with CHD are smoking, obesity, high blood cholesterol levels, hypertension (high blood pressure), lack of exercise, diabetes and a family history of premature heart disease. You can choose to stop smoking, get more exercise and *change your diet*. The U.S. Surgeon General has noted, "Of greatest concern is our excessive intake of dietary fat and its relationship to risk for chronic diseases, such as coronary heart disease, some types of cancer, diabetes, high blood pressure, strokes and obesity."

Most North Americans can benefit from a reduction in fat in their diet. Those at risk for CHD can benefit even more from aggressive dietary treatment. This cookbook does it *for* you! Low-fat cooking can be easy and delicious. You don't need to give up sauces and gravies; just learn how to prepare them the low-fat or no-fat way. Let this cookbook be your guide.

Low-fat cooking can help you lose weight. Why waste calories on hidden fat when you can enjoy fruit, vegetable, bread, pasta, fish and poultry dishes?

To help you watch your fat and your calories, the following recipes list calories, protein, fat, cholesterol, carbohydrates, fiber and sodium for each serving. These recipes are easy to prepare with ingredients that are readily available at your local supermarket.

Begin by reading labels. If a recipe calls for margarine, look for a margarine with reduced fat. These are called *diet margarines, imitation margarines* or *light margarines*. The USDA Handbook 8-4 says "Imitation margarines contain only about 40% fat and have about 17 calories per teaspoon. Regular soft-tub margarine contains about 34 calories per teaspoon and is almost 100% fat."

Diet or imitation margarines are your best choice to reduce your fat intake (and your calories!), but first check the type of fat in the margarine. You want one that contains corn, soybean, safflower or other vegetable oil. It should become quite soft when left at room temperature. Avoid those that contain coconut, palm or palm-kernel oil.

Just look on the label for saturated fat. You want to see the magic number 1 (gram) of saturated fat per serving. It will be one of the light soft margarines.

You can also find low-fat cheeses in many supermarkets. A listing of some low-fat cheeses is found on page 15. If you want to limit the amount of cheese in your diet, you won't have to give it up completely if you use these recipes and some common sense.

Recipes in this cookbook strictly limit fat. *Saturated fat* is animal fat but also includes coconut oil, palm oil and heavily hydrogenated vegetable fats that stay solid and hard at room temperature. Red meat, in general, has more fat than poultry and fish. Before preparation, skin poultry and remove all visible fat. This greatly reduces the fat otherwise found in poultry.

The section on herbs, page 17, gives you many ideas for seasoning foods without using butter or even diet margarine.

The National Cholesterol Education Program (NCEP) advocates a low-fat diet, where 30% or less of the calories come from fat, as the first line of treatment in reducing elevated blood cholesterol levels.

Of that 30% you will want to limit your saturated-fat intake to 10% of the total as a first step. If that does not produce the desired lowering of cholesterol, then use 7% of the total as saturated fat as a logical second step.

But what does this mean in terms of food and/or new methods of cooking and new recipes?

Calculating Your Fat Intake

Let's use the 30% goal as our guide and look at food intake. If you eat 1000 calories (kcal) a day, you should eat about 300kcal in fat. If you eat 2000kcal, fat should not account for more than 600kcal. That sounds easy enough, but fat has more than *twice* the number of calories (kcal/g) as carbohydrate or protein. Fat contains 9kcal/g; protein and carbohydrate have only 4kcal/g. Many of the protein foods you eat also contain fat. Meat and cheese are two examples.

So if you want to consume about 2000kcal a day and keep your fat intake to 30% of your calories, you must limit your *total* fat intake to about 66g of fat. That's just a little over 5 tablespoons, or a bit more than 1/2 a stick of butter or margarine. (This is for a *whole* day, and remember many foods contain fat!) Multiply the number of calories you wish to consume in a day by 30% (0.30) and divide the answer by 9 to get the number of *grams* of fat for that day. Example:

$$\frac{\text{Total calories X } 0.30}{9} = \frac{\text{Grams of fat}}{\text{for the day}}$$

Fat content on labels is listed in grams. But many foods contain "hidden fat." When fat is one of the first ingredients on a label, the food product is high in fat. It is easier to limit your fat intake if you don't eat a lot of pre-prepared foods.

Using this cookbook will really help because it lists the grams of fat per serving for every recipe.

This is probably more math than you want to deal with every day, so just keep track of two numbers: total calories and grams of saturated fat. You'll be on your way toward healthy eating. The chart below was taken from *Good Fat, Bad Fat: How to Lower Your Cholesterol and Beat the Odds of a Heart Attack by* Drs. Glen Griffin and William Castelli. This is another heart-healthy book from Fisher Books.

What Is Cholesterol?

Cholesterol is a fatty-like substance found in every cell in the human body. It is essential and is manufactured by the body. Most of the cholesterol in

Your caloric need:	10% of calories as saturated fat	7% of calories as saturated fat
1000 calories	11 grams	8 grams
1500 calories	17 grams	12 grams
2000 calories	22 grams	16 grams
2500 calories	28 grams	19 grams
3000 calories	33 grams	23 grams
4000 calories	44 grams	31 grams

your body is produced by the body when you eat an excessive amount of saturated fat.

Cholesterol is also in foods that come from animal sources. We call this *dietary cholesterol*. The body can produce all the cholesterol it needs for essential functions, so dietary cholesterol is not absolutely necessary. Excess dietary cholesterol may lead to increased blood cholesterol levels in some individuals.

Blood cholesterol is cholesterol that is being transported in the blood. It comes from both dietary sources and from the cholesterol the body makes. Cholesterol always travels from place to place mixed with protein particles called *lipoproteins*. The main lipoproteins that carry cholesterol are high-density lipoprotein (HDL) and low-density lipoprotein (LDL).

Atherosclerosis is the CHD disease that has created the need for cholesterol awareness. It begins with the accumulation of soft mounds of lipids (fats—primarily cholesterol) along the inner walls of the arteries. These mounds are called *plaque*. They gradually enlarge and eventually narrow the arteries and cause them to lose elasticity. When the blood flow is blocked, heart attack or stroke occurs. Most people have well-developed plaque by the time they are 30-years old. Recent research shows that reducing the amount of fat in the diet will reduce blood cholesterol. Other research shows that reducing blood cholesterol decreases the risk of atherosclerosis.

HDL vs LDL Cholesterol

Both HDL and LDL carry cholesterol in the blood, but there is a functional difference between them. LDL carries cholesterol *to* the body's cells. HDL takes up excess cholesterol from body tissues and cells and *returns* it to the liver for recycling or disposal. HDL picks up cholesterol from plaque deposits on artery walls, thereby reducing or minimizing the threat of atherosclerosis.

According to Dr. William Castelli, Director of the famed Framingham Heart Study, "It is extremely important to keep your HDL Cholesterol/Total Cholesterol ratio at a good or acceptable level. A ratio of 4.5 or less is beneficial. Ideally you would like to have your LDL cholesterol level below 130 and your total cholesterol level at under 200.

"People who reduce their cholesterol levels reduce their rate of heart attack and stroke. Plaque will stop growing in (and plugging up!) their arteries and if the cholesterol level is reduced far enough, the plaque will actually start going away."

What About Cholesterol?

For years we have been concerned about cholesterol because of its implications in CHD. In October, 1987, the National Heart, Lung, and Blood Institute (NHLBI) released new guidelines for treating high blood cholesterol and listed new risk categories that place as many as 40-million U.S. citizens in the "borderline" or "high-risk" categories for CHD.

Low-fat diets help most people lower their blood cholesterol. If you are obese, your body will make more cholesterol, regardless of the cholesterol you consume. A low-fat diet is an effective way to reduce obesity because it generally reduces caloric intake. A low-fat diet plays two roles in helping you lower your cholesterol and reduce your risk for CHD.

Every adult should know his/her cholesterol level, just as he/she should know his/her blood pressure. However, one measurement is not enough. Several are needed because most peo-

ple have a 5% variation in blood cholesterol levels and some have as much as a 20% variation. Also, there is a variation between laboratories and equipment. If you are tested and get a reading of over 200, be sure to have your total cholesterol level rechecked. If it still comes out over 200, get it checked a third time through your doctor or a lab that will provide total cholesterol and HDL and LDL cholesterol levels (called a *lipid profile*) so you can compute the ratios. Many counties or cities have cholesterol screenings available through public health departments that are reasonable and readily accessible. A blood cholesterol test is also usually part of a routine physical exam.

The NHLBI list a blood cholesterol level of 200-239mg/dl as being at *moderate risk*. If you have no other risk factors (smoking, hypertension, obesity, diabetes, no exercise and a family history of heart disease) and your blood cholesterol puts you in this group, monitor your cholesterol at least once a year. Follow the general dietary guidelines by reducing your overall fat intake to 30% of total calories. Also get a lipid profile. This will give you your Total Cholesterol/HDL Cholesterol ratio so you will have a better indication of actual CHD risk.

If you have a blood cholesterol level of 240mg/dl or above, you are considered to be at *high risk*. Get an appointment with your physician right away!

Your doctor will probably advise an aggressive dietary program. Limit your fat intake to *not more* than 30% of total calories. Limit your cholesterol intake.

These recipes are just what you need! Decrease saturated-fat intake and proportionately increase polyunsaturated-fat intake. Increase your dietary fiber intake and your fish consumption to 2 to 3 fish meals a week.

As a first step, your doctor will probably advise limiting cholesterol intake to 300mg/day with only 10% of your fat coming from saturated fat. *Saturated fat* is usually of animal origin, such as fat in meat, butter, cheese, poultry and fish. It also includes coconut and palm oils. *Unsaturated fats* include polyunsaturated fats and monounsaturated fats of plant origin, such as corn oil, safflower oil and olive oil. Further restrictions may involve lowering cholesterol intake to less than 200mg/day, with only 7% of total fat as saturated fat. A minimum of 6 months of intensive dietary therapy is usually recommended before any cholesterol-lowering drug therapy is started.

What Is Fiber?

Fiber is a general term for the components of plant-cell walls that cannot be digested in the human gastrointestinal (GI) tract. In the past, fiber in food was classified in terms of its crude-fiber content. Crude fiber was the indigestible substances left after food was digested in a test tube by harsh chemicals. Today we usually speak of *dietary fiber*. This is the fiber that resists human digestive enzymes and usually amounts to about 2 to 3 times as much as crude fiber.

Increasing dietary fiber in your diet is an excellent idea. Increasing dietary fiber usually means total fat in the diet is reduced. Soluble fibers, such as oat gum (found in rolled oats/oatmeal and oat bran), pectins (found in citrus fruits) and water-soluble fibers and gums from fruits, vegetables and legumes have been shown to reduce blood cholesterol levels.

Dietary fiber helps us in many ways. It prevents constipation by keeping the contents of the intestine moving and stimulates the muscles of the intestinal tract so they retain their health and tone, helping to prevent hemorrhoids and diverticulosis. Dietary fiber also promotes feelings of fullness and can help in reducing caloric intake because high-fiber foods absorb water but provide few calories. Increased dietary fiber intake is associated with a lower risk of colon cancer and helps people with diabetes by improving the body's handling of glucose.

Soluble fibers have been shown to reduce blood cholesterol—they enhance the clearance of cholesterol from the blood. Insoluble fibers (like wheat, corn and perhaps rice) are good in many ways. They have a laxative effect and thus seem to protect against bowel cancer—but they do not have as much cholesterol-lowering effect as soluble fibers. Both soluble and insoluble fibers have been part of diets which reduced cholesterol, but of the two, soluble seems to have the most cholesterol-lowering power.

The U.S. National Cancer Association recommends a high-fiber diet as a protective measure against colon cancer. Increasing your consumption of fruits, vegetables and whole grains such as oatmeal and oat bran, whole wheat and wheat bran and other whole-grain products is the easiest way to increase dietary fiber.

Certain foods may raise blood cholesterol. These include eggs, butter and animal fat.

Foods That Lower Cholesterol

We've already mentioned dietary fiber lowers cholesterol. Remember, the best way to increase your dietary fiber is by increasing your consumption of fruits, vegetables and whole grains.

Polyunsaturated fat and monounsaturated fat also lower cholesterol. Olive oil is a good example of a monounsaturated vegetable oil. That's why you'll find a small amount of olive oil in a number of recipes in this cookbook. Fish (especially salmon, sardines, mackerel, herring and trout), legumes, textured soy protein (TVP), soy milk and non-fat milk have also demonstrated cholesterol-lowering effects. Garlic appears to lower cholesterol and LDL while raising HDL. The quantities of garlic needed to provide this effect are substantial (1 whole bulb per day) and may have other side effects like gastric distress and unpleasant body odor.

Optimal intakes of vitamins and minerals are necessary to keep cholesterol normal and prevent atherosclerosis. The best way to get the vitamins and minerals you need is by eating a well balanced varied diet. Supplementation is not usually necessary, but if you do supplement, take only one balanced vitamin-mineral capsule a day. You will want to choose one that provides *all* the RDA nutrients in amounts smaller than, equal to or very close to the RDA.

If you want to lower your cholesterol with diet, eat a balanced and varied low-fat, calorie-controlled, low-cholesterol diet. Eat more vegetables, fruit and whole grains (especially oats) and legumes, use skim milk and low-fat yogurt, season with herbs, garlic, onions and hot peppers. Use monounsaturated oils such as olive oil, peanut oil, canola (Puritan®) and polyunsaturated oils such as safflower, corn, sunflower, cottonseed or soybean oil in your food preparation.

To keep your diet well-balanced you need 4 or more servings of fruits and vegetables each day and at least 4 servings of whole-grain bread or cereal products. Eat 2 or more servings of low-fat dairy products and 2 servings of fish, poultry or legumes each day. Variety is not only the spice of life, it is also the key to healthful nutrition.

Exercise, Stress and Cholesterol

There is good scientific evidence that exercise will help reduce high blood cholesterol. It does this in several ways, one is by reducing obesity. Studies of other populations who have low blood cholesterol levels yet consume a high-fat and high-cholesterol diet suggest that exercise is a major factor influencing blood cholesterol levels and reducing CHD risk. It is certainly reasonable to incorporate a regular exercise program into your life style. Exercise can be fun. Biking, dancing (like square dancing), swimming, tennis (particularly a fast-paced singles match) and running are all good aerobic exercise. Still, the simplest and safest exercise you can participate in may be brisk walking.

Stress adversely affects blood cholesterol levels. An additional effect of exercise is to help *reduce* stress. Other mechanisms for reducing stress are relaxation techniques, meditation or prayer and play time.

Eat a healthy varied diet and *enjoy* it. Exercise daily, relax, meditate or pray, play, have fun and enjoy life. Happy people have lower blood cholesterol levels!

Helpful Hints

You can substitute oat bran for some of the flour in most of the recipes in this cookbook. Try substituting 1/4 cup oat bran for 1/4 cup flour in a recipe that calls for 1 cup flour: use 3/4 cup flour and 1/4 cup oat bran. Some recipes already use oat bran or oatmeal.

It's easy to sauté foods with almost no fat. Spraying a pan lightly with a vegetable non-stick spray or wiping it with olive oil will allow you to sauté or even brown many foods. You don't need a lot of oil or butter.

Many sauces can be made with minimal or no fat. Instead of making the typical roux (1/2 fat, 1/2 flour), use cornstarch as the thickening agent. It takes only 1/2 the amount of cornstarch as flour to thicken a product.

To prepare a low-fat gravy, use fat-free broth, season to taste, bring to a boil and add cornstarch by mixing it with cold water until a thin suspension has formed. Pour the mixture into the hot liquid and heat until it becomes translucent and comes to a boil If the gravy is not thick enough, add more cornstarch in the same way.

White sauces can be made the same way. Just use low-fat or skim milk and thicken with cornstarch. A trick to make a "creamier" white sauce without adding fat is to add a tablespoon or two of dry non-fat milk to the low-fat or skim milk before preparing the white sauce.

Herbs, spices and seasonings can play a major role in making foods tasty and appetizing.

—Ann Tinsley

What About Children?

Children should avoid extremes in their diet unless their family history and blood cholesterol levels indicate an unusually high hereditary risk. Most children should eat a diet where 30% to 40% of their calories comes from fat.

You don't have to cook separately for the children in your family when you use these recipes. Children should consume three to four 8-ounce glasses of whole milk or 2% milk every day. Add a bit more olive oil to their salads and you'll easily achieve 30% or more of their calories coming from fat. You can do this easily with little extra effort.

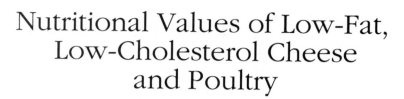

Nutritional Values of Low-Fat, Low-Cholesterol Cheese and Poultry

	Cal kcal	Prot gm	Fat gm	Chol mg	Carb gm	Sod mg

Cheese   1 oz. serving

Pre Monde

	Cal kcal	Prot gm	Fat gm	Chol mg	Carb gm	Sod mg
	97	7	8	25	4	95

Alpine Lace

Swiss

	100	n/a	8	25	n/a	35

American

	80	n/a	7	20	n/a	200

Cheddar

	97	n/a	8	25	n/a	90

Muenster

	104	n/a	8	25	n/a	85

Provolone

	100	n/a	6.8	20	n/a	85

Lifetime Natural Cheeses

Swiss

	55	7	3	15	trace	35

Monterey Jack

	55	7	3	20	trace	75

Dorman's Light Low-Chol (imitation)

Munster

	70	6	5	3	n/a	190

Kraft Light 'n' Lively

American flavor

	70	6	4	15	2	300

New Holland Hot Jalapeño

	90	7	8	n/a	1	100

	Cal kcal	Prot gm	Fat gm	Chol mg	Carb gm	Sod mg

Regular Cheddar (for comparison)

	114	7	9	30	trace	176

Cottage Cheese

2%

	25	4	.5	2	1	115

1%

	20	3.5	trace	1	1	115

Ricotta (Part Skim)

	25	3.5	2.5	10	1.5	39

Mozzarella (Part Skim)

	72	7	5	16	1	132

Parmesan (grated) 1 T.

	23	2.1	1.5	4	.2	93

This information is current as of this printing. Check manufacturer's label for updated analysis.

Poultry

Chicken   raw, no skin

1/2 breast

	129	27	1	0	68	76	0

1 leg

	156	26	5	0	112	104	0

Turkey   flesh only, raw

100 g edible portion, (about 3 1/2 oz.)

	110	22	2	0	73	61	0

Nutritional Values of Various Fin and Shellfish

Cal Kcal	Prot gm	Fat gm	Chol mg	Carb gm	Sodium mg
Bass, freshwater					
3 oz. raw					
97	16	3	58	0	59
Catfish, channel					
3 oz. raw					
99	15	4	49	0	54
Cod, Atlantic					
3 oz. raw					
70	15	1	37	0	46
Mahi Mahi, dolphinfish					
3 oz. raw					
73	16	1	62	0	74
Flounder & sole					
3 oz. raw					
78	16	1	41	0	69
Haddock					
3 oz. raw					
74	16	1	49	0	58
Halibut					
3 oz. raw					
93	18	2	27	0	46
Monkfish					
3 oz. raw					
64	12	1	21	0	16
Perch, ocean					
3 oz. raw					
60	12	1	27	0	48
Salmon, pink					
3 oz. raw					
99	17	3	44	0	57

Cal Kcal	Prot gm	Fat gm	Chol mg	Carb gm	Sodium mg
Salmon, sockeye					
3 oz. canned					
130	17	6	37	0	458
Snapper					
3 oz. raw					
85	17	1	31	0	54
Trout					
3 oz. raw					
126	18	6	49	0	44
Tuna, white					
3 oz. canned in water					
116	23	2	35	0	333
Crab meat, Alaska King					
3 oz. cooked					
82	16	1	45	0	911
Imitation crab (Surim!)					
3 oz.					
87	10	1	17	9	715
***Shrimp**					
3 oz. raw					
90	17	2	130	1	126
Clams					
3 oz. raw					
63	11	1	29	2	47
Oysters, Eastern					
3 oz. raw					
58	6	2	46	3	94

* Note: Shrimp is naturally high in cholesterol.

Source: "Composition of Foods: Finfish and Shellfish Products," Agriculture Handbook Number 8-15, USDA Human Nutrition Information Service, Revised September, 1987.

Herbs & Spices

Herbs are plants that are used for flavoring or garnishing in cooking, for medicinal purposes and for making perfumes and potpourris. Charlemagne described an herb as, "The friend of the physician and the pride of cooks."

Herbs are very helpful in salt-free diets. Even though my family is not required to be on a salt-free diet, I enjoy cooking with herbs, and I often experiment with different combinations. As a gardener, they are some of my favorite plants to grow.

Herbs may be used fresh or dried. When using fresh herbs, they are not as potent, so you need to use more. Cut fresh herbs very fine with kitchen shears to help blend their flavor with the food.

Here are some suggestions for using herbs in your cooking:

Anise (licorice-flavored seeds)—Use to flavor many dishes, casseroles, vegetables, cookies or cakes. Store sugar in an air tight container overnight with anise seeds, then use the sugar on sugar cookies, pancakes or hot toast. If you don't want anise seeds in your food, use anisette, an anise-flavored liqueur.

Basil—Use with fish, Italian dishes, chicken, fresh tomatoes, squash, peas, carrots, cauliflower, salads and tomatoes. Or make your own basil vinegar.

Bay leaves—Use in beans, soups, chicken, rice and cooked red cabbage. Always remove the leaf before serving because it is unpalatable.

Burnet—Use in salads and salad dressings.

Chervil—Use in soup, salads and sauces. (Has sort of an anise flavor.)

Chives—Use in chowder, chicken, tuna, salads, mashed potatoes, soups, zucchini, bread dough, vegetable dips or sprinkle over fresh tomatoes.

Cilantro—Use in salads, Mexican foods, salsa and soups. Cilantro has a distinctive flavor, so use with caution.

Coriander—Use with apple pie or other apple dishes and sugar cookies.

Dill—Use in biscuits, rolls or any

homemade bread, salads, freshly sliced cucumbers, fresh tomatoes, vegetable dips, asparagus, green beans, cooked potatoes, potato salad, beets or fish. Or make your own dill vinegar.

Garlic—Use in vegetable dips, chicken, Italian dishes, Mexican dishes, fish and soup.

Ginger—Use with carrots or in gingerbread. Also use fresh for stir-fried dishes. Substitute fresh ginger in recipes that call for ground ginger; use about half the amount called for.

Marjoram—Use with zucchini, soup, chicken and biscuits. Sprinkle over fresh tomatoes—basic in Italian dishes.

Mints—Use in peas, pea soup, fruit or as a garnish for iced tea.

Oregano—Use in bread dough, Italian dishes, Mexican dishes and with zucchini.

Parsley—Use in salads, bread dough, new potatoes, creamed potatoes, vegetable dips, soup, rice, fish, meat balls and chicken.

Rosemary—Use in chicken, biscuits, stuffing, green beans and rice.

Sage—Use in chicken, meat loaf, rice, stuffing and gravy.

Tarragon—Use with fish, chicken, in sauces, vegetable dips, salad or green beans. Or make your own tarragon vinegar.

Thyme—Use in chicken, stuffing, rice,

beets, carrots and green beans.

Herb vinegar

Herb vinegar is easy to make and fun to experiment with. As a general rule, put 1 cup fresh, clean herbs in a glass 1-quart jar. Add enough vinegar to cover the herbs. Cover and let steep for about 2 weeks. Check occasionally to be sure all the herb's are covered by vinegar. If not, add more vinegar.

The longer you let the vinegar and herbs steep, the stronger the flavor. When you are pleased with the flavor, strain the vinegar.

To avoid the chance of a chemical reaction, only use glass jars with non-metal tops, such as decanters or wine bottles.

Bouquet garni

Bouquet garni is generally used in soups, stews or foods that must be cooked for a long period. It is also used in recipes where you want the flavor without any bits of herbs. Tie herbs in a piece of cheesecloth and add to the food. When finished cooking, remove the bag and discard.

You can use any combination of herbs for a bouquet garni, or keep the traditional combination on hand. It calls for bay leaf, parsley, marjoram and thyme. I also like to add one or two garlic cloves.

Spices

Spices are commonly used to flavor food. They have a strong, pungent flavor. Unlike herbs, which can be easily grown in home gardens, spices are usually imported. The aroma always conjures up foreign, exotic places in my mind.

Below are some suggestions for using spices in your cooking.

Allspice—Use with chicken crepes, fruit crepes, fresh fruit, rice pudding, fruit dips, marinara sauce and French toast.

Black pepper—Whole pepper-corns, freshly ground, are very pungent. Ground black pepper loses its punch faster. Use in meat and vegetable dishes.

Cayenne pepper—Made from the hottest chili peppers, which are small and vary in color from yellow to red. Use with chicken, beans, Mexican dishes and barbecue sauce.

Lemon pepper—Blend of dried lemon-rind and ground black pepper.

Use with chicken, fish, dips and sea-food chowder.

Red pepper—Made from larger, less-pungent (but still hot) peppers. Use in chicken, fish, dried beans, Mexican and Italian dishes.

Chili powder—Blend of chili peppers, oregano, cumin, garlic powder, salt and onion powder. Use with chicken, dried beans and Mexican dishes.

Cinnamon—Use with blueberries, apple dishes, pumpkin, peaches, cherries, fruit salad, fruit dips, cakes, gingerbread, cookies, pies, rice pudding and French toast.

Cloves—Use with pumpkin, apple, fruit salad, fruit dips, chicken salad, red cabbage and French toast.

Curry powder—Blend of several pungent, exotic spices. Use with chicken, seafood, rice, cocktail sauces and dips.

Nutmeg—Use with sweet potatoes, pumpkin, spinach, quiche, peas, carrots, sauces, fruit pies and rice pudding.

Paprika—Sprinkle on fish, chicken or vegetables. Adds a dash of color as well as flavor.

Saffron—Very expensive, but it goes a long way. Use with chicken and rice.

Turmeric—Use with salads, coleslaw and chicken. Also good to add a bit of yellow coloring to foods.

Special Menus

Brunch

Variety of chilled juices
Fresh-Fruit Kabobs, page 45
Miniature Crab Quiche, page 41
Mixed green salad
Sweet & Sour Dressing, page 119
Blueberry Tea Cake, page 263
Tea or coffee

Special-Occasion Breakfast

Grapefruit half
French Toast with Steamed Apples,
    page 85
Maple syrup
Skim milk
Tea or coffee

Weekday Breakfast

Chilled orange juice
Cornflakes sprinkled with Bran Buds®
1/2 banana, sliced over cereal
Oat-Bran Muffin, page 68

Any-Day Breakfast

Orange slices
Scrambled Egg Beaters®
Whole-wheat toast
Strawberry jelly

Breakfast for a Cold Winter Day

Steamed prunes
Oatmeal
Raisin-bread toast
Skim milk

Saturday Breakfast

Grapefruit juice
Pancakes, page 83
Maple syrup
Skim milk

Ladies' Luncheon

Curried Chicken & Pasta Salad,
  page 111
Fresh melon wedges
Whole-Wheat Molasses Bread, page 75
Lemon Snow Pudding, page 296
Hot tea

Lunch for a Summer Day

Tuna-salad sandwich
Honey Whole-Wheat Bread, page 77
Pickled Beets & Onions, page 109
Pineapple-Cherry Sherbet, page 118
Iced tea

Lunch for a Cold Day

Corn Chips, page 40
Chicken Chili, page 147
Spinach salad
John's Favorite Dressing, page 118
Fresh orange wedges
Hot tea

Lunch for the Garden Club

Assorted fresh vegetables
Herb Dip, page 34
Tropical Tuna Salad, page 98
Oatmeal Muffins, page 70
Spiced iced tea with lemon wedge

Meatless Lunch

Vegetable Tostadas, page 192
Assorted fresh fruit
Fresh-Fruit Dip, page 32

Prepare-Ahead Lunch

Potato-Leek Soup, page 62
Chipped-Turkey Sandwiches, page 249
Carrot sticks
Fresh fruit

Week-day Dinner

Coleslaw, page 94
Salmon Patties, page 174
Rice & Green Onion, page 216
Glazed Carrots & Zucchini, page 207
Corn Bread, page 72
Apples & Cranberries, page 285

Dinner for a Busy Day
(Prepare the entire meal the day
before)

Assorted fresh vegetables
Tarragon-Vegetable Dip, page 37
Frozen-Cabbage Salad, page 101
Chicken & Vegetable Casserole,
  page 136
Dilly Bread, page 76

Italian Dinner

Spicy Garbanzo Beans, page 43
Pasta with Chicken, page 144
Mixed green salad
No-oil Italian dressing
Hot Garlic Bread, page 79
Fresh fruit
Wine

Meatless Dinner

Stuffed Cherry Tomatoes, page 44
Vegetarian Lasagna, page 189
Mixed green salad
Vinegar & Oil Dressing, page 121
Rye bread
Baked Pears & Raisins, page 290

Dinner In A Hurry

Sliced tomatoes
So-easy Fish, page 163
Oven French Fries, page 214
Vegetable combination (frozen foods)
French bread
Fresh fruit
Fresh-Fruit Dip, page 32

Casual-Company Dinner

Pumpernickel-Spinach Dip, page 36
Mixed green salad
No-oil Italian dressing
Chicken Stuffed Pasta Shells, page 146
Jean's Italian Bread, page 78
Blueberry & Peach Crisp, page 286
White wine

Dinner on the Grill

Pennsylvania Dutch Tomatoes & Onions,
    page 113
Grilled Salmon, page 180
Corn on the cob
Sourdough rolls
Rice Pudding, page 297

Special-Company Dinner

Fresh vegetables
Horseradish Dip, page 33
Sparkling Fruit Cup, page 104
Coq au Vin, page 130
Brown-Rice Pilaf, page 200
Petite peas
Dinner Rolls, page 80
White wine

Thanksgiving Dinner

Cranberry-Orange Salad, page 103
Roast turkey
Chicken Gravy, page 229
Mashed potatoes
Pennsylvania Sweet Potatoes in Tangy
   Sauce, page 213
Succotash
Dinner Rolls, page 80
Apples & Cranberries, page 285
Whipped Topping, page 304

Hawaiian Buffet

Audrey's Oriental Chicken, page 151
Brown-Rice Pilaf, page 200
Gingered Carrots, page 205
Mixed Fruit with Coconut Pudding,
   page 91
Green Beans & Dill, page 196
Hot crispy rolls
Piña Colada Crepes, page 306

Easter Buffet

Sparkling Fruit Cup, page 104
Asparagus Salad, page 99
Baked turkey breast
New potatoes with parsley
Fresh green peas
Homemade Biscuits, page 66
Pineapple-Cherry Upside-Down Cake,
   page 269

Christmas-Eve Supper

Sylvia's Orange-Gelatin Salad, page 107
Chicken-Vegetable Soup with Herb
   Dumplings, page 55
Hot crusty bread
Assorted holiday cookies

Summer Sunday Supper

Fresh-Fruit Kabobs, page 45
Grilled-Chicken Sandwiches,
   page 252
Grandma's Potato Salad, page 110
Oatmeal Muffins, page 70
Lemonade

Winter Sunday Supper

Waldorf Salad, page 115
Clam-Corn Chowder, page 56
Best Oatmeal Cookies, page 273
Hot spiced tea

Appetizers

I have created appetizers that are both nutritious and appealing. No longer will you have to be concerned about appetizers and snacks that are high in all the "no-nos."

Children who are not particularly fond of fresh fruit suddenly can't get enough when they have Fresh-Fruit Dip to "dunk" the fruit in. They also love the Corn Chips hot from the oven and Quesadillas with warm melted low-fat cheese. Keep a basket of fresh fruit on the table or within easy reach. Colorful and fresh fruit appeals to children *and* adults.

For nourishing, quick additions to lunch box or an afterschool snack, fill attractive glass jars with carrot sticks, celery sticks and zucchini wedges. Keep them in the refrigerator for snackers. To serve the same purpose, keep a supply of small rice cakes and crisp flat breads in the cabinet. Most children are just as happy to munch on these feather-light snacks as on cholesterol-heavy crackers. Read every label to make sure snacks conform to your diet.

Give your family a variety of nutritious foods to choose from, and make all these foods easy to see and reach.

Following are appetizers that can be prepared and presented in a minimum of time.

❧ Try thinly sliced smoked turkey breast, served on crisp flat bread, garnished with a tiny sweet pickle.

❧ If your diet permits smoked oysters, try cherry tomatoes stuffed with smoked oysters that have been dipped in seafood sauce.

❧ Imitation crab is a versatile addition to your menu. You don't have to put forth much effort for this delicious treat. Serve imitation crab on wooden picks with seafood sauce.

❧ For a simple, hot appetizer, prepare Cathy's Baked Chicken, page 129, but first cut the chicken breast in finger-size strips then continue with the original recipe.

Appetizers are to stimulate the appetite, not satisfy it. How many times have you spent days preparing for a dinner party only to watch your guests indulge in too many appetizers and not be hungry for the remainder of the meal? Watch the quantity, don't make too many and don't pass them around too many times.

Marinated Vegetables

Works well on your favorite vegetables.

3 cups prepared vegetables of choice

5 slices red onion

1/2 cup no-oil Italian dressing

1 teaspoon chopped pimiento

1/4 teaspoon celery seed

1/2 teaspoon Italian seasoning

Use your favorite vegetable or a combination such as:
  Broccoli
  Cauliflower
  Mushrooms
  Zucchini chunks

In a medium saucepan or saucepans, steam vegetables of choice until barely tender; remove to a medium-size bowl. Separate onion slices into rings; mix into vegetables. In a small bowl, combine dressing, pimiento, celery seed and Italian seasoning. Mix well and pour over vegetables. Cover and refrigerate several hours or overnight. Arrange vegetables attractively on a serving platter with wooden picks available.

Yield: 12 (1/4-cup) servings

1 serving contains:

Cal	Prot	Fat	Chol	Carb	Fib	Sodium
12kc	1gm	trace	0	2gm	1gm	24mg

Garbanzo-Bean Spread

Attractive and tasty when spread on celery or other vegetables.

1 (15-oz.) can garbanzo beans, drained, 1 tablespoon liquid reserved

1 garlic clove, minced

1 teaspoon oil of choice

1 teaspoon lime juice

Dash of red-pepper sauce

2 tablespoons plain low-fat yogurt

2 tablespoons chopped pimiento

Salt and pepper to taste

In a medium bowl, combine beans, 1 tablespoon bean liquid, garlic, oil and lime juice. In a blender or food processor fitted with the metal blade, process mixture until smooth; it may be necessary to process in two batches if using a blender. Scoop into bowl. Stir in Tabasco, yogurt, pimiento, salt and pepper. Serve as desired.

Yield: 20 (1-tablespoon) servings

1 serving contains:

Cal	Prot	Fat	Chol	Carb	Fib	Sodium
24kc	1gm	1gm	trace	4gm	1gm	110mg

Refried-Bean Dip

*A tasty addition to your next barbecue.
Serve warm with Corn Chips, page 40,
or raw vegetables.*

2 cups Refried Beans, page 203

1/4 cup chopped onion

2 tablespoons chopped green chilies

1/2 cup salsa

In a medium-size saucepan, combine all
ingredients. Heat over medium heat
until bubbling. Or use a microwave
oven. Serve as desired.

Yield: 18 (2-tablespoon) servings

1 serving contains:

Cal	Prot	Fat	Chol	Carb	Fib	Sodium
7kc	trace	trace	trace	1gm	trace	27mg

Zippy Meat Balls

This special treat uses ground turkey.

1 lb. ground raw turkey

About 1 cup fresh bread crumbs

1/3 cup minced onion

2 egg whites, slightly beaten

1 tablespoon minced fresh parsley

Pepper to taste

1/2 teaspoon Worcestershire sauce

1/2 teaspoon olive oil

Sauce:

1 (12-oz.) bottle chili sauce

1 (10-oz.) jar grape jelly

1/4 teaspoon ground ginger

In a large bowl, combine turkey, bread crumbs, onion, egg whites, parsley, pepper and Worcestershire sauce. This mixture needs to be fairly firm, so add more bread crumbs if needed. Shape into 1-inch balls. Heat a large non-stick skillet, add oil, then meatballs. Cook until done, turning gently to brown on all sides. Drain. To make the sauce, combine chili sauce, jelly and ginger in a medium-size saucepan. Heat over medium-low heat until jelly is melted, stirring constantly. Add meat balls; stir gently to coat all sides. Simmer, uncovered, 30 minutes. Serve in an ovenproof dish set on a heating tray with wooden picks.

Yield: About 17 (2-meat-ball) servings

1 serving contains:

Cal	Prot	Fat	Chol	Carb	Fib	Sodium
115kc	5gm	1gm	11mg	22mg	trace	333mg

Spinach-Seafood Pizza

Serve as an appetizer or prepare in a round pizza pan and cut in wedges for lunch.

Cornmeal

1/2 recipe Pizza Dough, page 190

1 teaspoon oil of choice

1 (10-oz.) pkg. thawed frozen chopped spinach, well-drained

1/2 teaspoon dried leaf tarragon

About 8 oz. imitation crab, chopped in medium-size chunks

2 cups (8 oz.) shredded part-skim-milk mozzarella cheese

Lightly spray a 13" x 9" pan lightly with vegetable spray and sprinkle with cornmeal. Pat pizza dough into prepared pan. Let rest 20 minutes. Preheat oven to 425F (220C). Brush oil over dough. Squeeze excess moisture from spinach using several layers of paper towel. Spread spinach evenly over dough; sprinkle tarragon over spinach. Spread crabmeat over spinach; sprinkle with cheese. Bake 15 to 18 minutes or until cheese is browned and bubbling. Cut into 24 squares and serve immediately.

Yield: 24 servings

1 serving contains:

Cal	Prot	Fat	Chol	Carb	Fib	Sodium
66kc	5gm	2gm	8mg	7gm	1gm	109mg

Fresh-Fruit Dip

Delicious accompaniment for fresh fruit.

1 cup plain low-fat yogurt

1 tablespoon honey

1/8 teaspoon ground nutmeg

1/8 teaspoon ground allspice

In a small bowl, combine all ingredients; refrigerate. Serve as a dip with fresh fruit.

Yield: 16 (1-tablespoon) servings

1 serving contains:

Cal	Prot	Fat	Chol	Carb	Fib	Sodium
13kc	1gm	trace	1mg	2gm	0	10mg

Variations:

Indian-Fruit Dip: Substitute 1/8 teaspoon ground ginger and 1/8 teaspoon ground cloves for spices.

Almond-Fruit Dip: Omit honey and spices. Combine 1 package artificial sweetener and 1/2 teaspoon almond flavoring with yogurt.

Coconut-Fruit Dip: Omit honey and spices. Combine 1 package artificial sweetener and 1/2 teaspoon coconut flavoring with yogurt.

Horseradish Dip

Horseradish and mustard combination creates a perky taste.

1 cup Sour-Cream Substitute, page 241

3/4 cup low-fat mayonnaise-type salad dressing

1/2 teaspoon Worcestershire sauce

1-1/2 teaspoons grated onion

1 teaspoon dry mustard

1 teaspoon snipped chives or to taste

3/4 teaspoon prepared horseradish

1/2 teaspoon lemon pepper

1/2 teaspoon garlic powder

1 teaspoon parsley flakes

In a small bowl, combine all ingredients. Cover and refrigerate several hours. Serve as desired.

Yield: 28 (1-tablespoon) servings

1 serving contains:

Cal	Prot	Fat	Chol	Carb	Fib	Sodium
15kc	1gm	1gm	1mg	1gm	trace	55mg

Herb Dip

Sour cream with dill makes it special.

**1 cup Sour-Cream Substitute,
   page 241**

**3/4 cup low-fat mayonnaise-type
   salad dressing**

1 teaspoon grated onion

1 teaspoon parsley flakes

1 teaspoon snipped chives

1/2 teaspoon dill weed

1/8 teaspoon garlic powder

In a small bowl, combine all ingredients. Cover and refrigerate several hours. Serve as desired.

Yield: 28 (1-tablespoon) servings

1 serving contains:

Cal	Prot	Fat	Chol	Carb	Fib	Sodium
15kc	1gm	1gm	1mg	1gm	trace	61mg

Crab Dip

An impressive, delicious low-fat dip.
Serve hot or chilled with Corn Chips,
page 40, or small rice cakes.

**1 cup Sour-Cream Substitute,
  page 241**

**1/2 cup low-fat mayonnaise-type
  salad dressing**

1/2 teaspoon lemon juice

1/8 teaspoon garlic powder

1/8 teaspoon dill weed

1/8 teaspoon lemon pepper

**4 oz. imitation crab, cut into small
  chunks**

Dash of paprika

Preheat oven to 400F (205C). In a
medium bowl, combine all ingredients
except paprika. Spoon mixture into a
1-quart shallow baking dish. Sprinkle
with paprika. Bake in conventional
oven 20 minutes or just until heated. Or
microwave on HIGH 5 minutes. Serve
as desired.

Yield: 12 (1/4-cup) servings

1 serving contains:

Cal	Prot	Fat	Chol	Carb	Fib	Sodium
48kc	5gm	2gm	2mg	2gm	trace	130mg

Pumpernickel-Spinach Dip

Fun party food.

1 lb. round loaf pumpernickel bread

1 cup Sour-Cream Substitute, page 241

3/4 cup low-fat mayonnaise-type salad dressing

1 (8-oz.) can water chestnuts, drained, finely chopped

1/2 cup minced onion

1 pkg. Knorr's® vegetable soup mix

1 teaspoon parsley flakes

1 (10-oz.) pkg. thawed frozen chopped spinach, well-drained

Cut top off loaf and carefully remove most of bread inside, leaving a shell. In a large bowl, combine remaining ingredients. Cover and refrigerate several hours. To serve, spoon filling into hollowed-out loaf of bread. Serve with remaining bread, cut in cubes.

Yield: 16 (1/4-cup) servings

1 serving contains:

Cal	Prot	Fat	Chol	Carb	Fib	Sodium
120kc	5gm	3gm	2mg	20gm	2gm	333mg

Tarragon-Vegetable Dip

A favorite of our gang in Newburg, Indiana.

1/2 cup low-fat mayonnaise-type salad dressing

1/2 cup Sour-Cream Substitute, page 241

1 teaspoon tarragon vinegar

1/2 teaspoon garlic powder

1/4 teaspoon curry powder

1/2 teaspoon prepared horseradish

1/2 teaspoon onion powder

In a small bowl, combine all ingredients. Cover and refrigerate several hours. Serve as desired.

Yield: 16 (1-tablespoon) servings

1 serving contains:

Cal	Prot	Fat	Chol	Carb	Fib	Sodium
16kc	1gm	1gm	1mg	1gm	0	53mg

Turkey Spread

Delicious served with small rice cakes.
Or try it as a tasty sandwich filling.

1/2 cup low-fat cottage cheese

1/2 cup plain low-fat yogurt

1/2 cup low-fat mayonnaise-type salad dressing

1 teaspoon minced onion

1 teaspoon parsley flakes

1/2 teaspoon dill weed

1/2 teaspoon garlic powder

7 oz. turkey, white meat, cooked, cut into chunks

Parsley sprigs to garnish

In a blender or food processor fitted with the metal blade, blend cottage cheese and yogurt until smooth. Pour into a medium bowl and stir in salad dressing, onion, parsley, dill weed and garlic powder. In a food processor, process turkey with the on/off switch until chopped very fine, about the consistency of ground meat. Stir turkey into cottage-cheese mixture. Cover and refrigerate several hours. Garnish with parsley sprigs and serve as desired.

Yield: 10 (1/4-cup) servings

Serving suggestions:

Spread over small rice cakes and arrange on a serving tray lined with lettuce.
Spread on party-size bread, cut into quarters for bite-size pieces.

1 serving contains:

Cal	Prot	Fat	Chol	Carb	Fib	Sodium
63kc	8gm	3gm	17mg	3gm	trace	102mg

Grace's Chicken Wings

So good you won't be able to stop with just one!

24 chicken wings, about 3 lbs.

1 cup sugar

3 tablespoons cornstarch

1/2 teaspoon ground ginger

1/4 teaspoon grated lemon peel

1/4 teaspoon pepper

1/8 teaspoon onion powder

3/4 cup water

1/3 cup lemon juice

1/4 cup soy sauce

Lemon slices to garnish

Preheat oven to 400F (205C). Using kitchen shears, cut drumette from remainder of wing on each piece of chicken. (Drumette is the largest section of the chicken wing.) Save scrappy pieces for broth. Place chicken drumettes on a broiler pan with a rack. Bake 25 minutes. In a saucepan, combine sugar and cornstarch; add ginger, lemon peel, pepper, onion powder, water, lemon juice and soy sauce. Cook over medium heat until mixture starts to simmer; cook 3 to 4 minutes longer. Pour sauce over chicken. Cover and refrigerate until almost serving time. Bake in preheated 400F (205C) oven 30 minutes until browned and heated. Serve garnished with lemon slices in an ovenproof dish set on a heating tray.

Yield: 24 servings

1 serving contains:

Cal	Prot	Fat	Chol	Carb	Fib	Sodium
135kc	9gm	7gm	29mg	9gm	trace	200mg

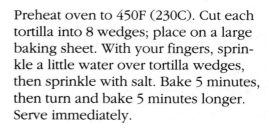

Corn Chips

Serve this low-fat snack alone or with your favorite dip or salsa.

8 (6-inch) corn tortillas (made with corn oil or without lard)

Water

Seasoned salt to taste

Preheat oven to 450F (230C). Cut each tortilla into 8 wedges; place on a large baking sheet. With your fingers, sprinkle a little water over tortilla wedges, then sprinkle with salt. Bake 5 minutes, then turn and bake 5 minutes longer. Serve immediately.

Yield: 4 (1-cup) servings

These tortillas can be found in most grocery stores. Just read the label and make certain they are made with a permissible oil.

1 serving contains:

Cal	Prot	Fat	Chol	Carb	Fib	Sodium
134kc	4gm	2gm	0	26gm	2gm	166mg

Miniature Crab Quiche

Avoids the high cholesterol of traditional quiche.

Pastry dough for 1 pie crust made with corn oil, page 295

1 egg white

1/4 cup egg substitute

1/4 cup skimmed evaporated milk

1/4 cup shredded low-fat Swiss cheese

1 tablespoon minced green onion, green and white parts

1/8 teaspoon salt

1/8 teaspoon ground marjoram

1/8 teaspoon ground lemon pepper

1/2 cup finely chopped imitation crab

1/4 cup grated Parmesan cheese

Preheat oven to 400F (205C). Lightly grease two pans of miniature muffin cups (24 muffins cups). Roll pastry dough between two sheets of wax paper until quite thin. Using a 2-1/2-inch round cutter, cut dough into circles and fit into miniature muffin cups. Prick crusts. Bake 2 minutes, prick again and bake 2 minutes longer. Remove crusts from oven; reduce oven temperature to 350F (175C). Combine egg white, egg substitute, evaporated milk, cheese, green onion, salt, marjoram, lemon pepper and imitation crab in a medium bowl. Spoon mixture into miniature quiche crusts; sprinkle with Parmesan cheese. Bake about 20 minutes or until set. Let set in pan 5 minutes before carefully removing to a serving tray.

Yield: 24 servings (1 quiche each)

1 serving contains:

Cal	Prot	Fat	Chol	Carb	Fib	Sodium
60kc	3gm	3gm	2mg	5gm	trace	69mg

Nachos

*Great addition to a Mexican-style
dinner.*

**8 (6-inch) corn tortillas (made with
corn oil or without lard)**

**3/4 cup shredded low-fat cheddar
cheese**

3 tablespoons salsa

Preheat oven to 400F (205C). Cut each
tortilla into 8 wedges; place on a large
baking sheet. Bake about 5 minutes,
turn and bake 5 minutes longer or until
crisp. Sprinkle cheese evenly over
chips, then lightly sprinkle salsa over
cheese. Bake 4 to 5 minutes longer or
until cheese is melted.

Yield: 4 (1-cup) servings

1 serving contains:

Cal	Prot	Fat	Chol	Carb	Fib	Sodium
198kc	11gm	6gm	15mg	28gm	2gm	306mg

Variation

For extra spice, add a few thin slices of
jalapeño pepper on top of salsa.

Spicy Garbanzo Beans

High-fiber, low-fat substitute for peanuts.

1 (15-oz.) can garbanzo beans

1/4 teaspoon freshly ground black pepper

Dash of paprika or to taste

Drain beans thoroughly. Lay on paper towel and pat dry. Sprinkle with black pepper and paprika. Set around in bowls to munch on instead of nuts.

Yield: 6 (1/4-cup) servings

1 serving contains:

Cal	Prot	Fat	Chol	Carb	Fib	Sodium
70kc	3gm	1gm	0	12gm	3gm	282mg

Stuffed Cherry Tomatoes

Rich in vitamins, low in fat.

25 cherry tomatoes, about 1 lb., washed, dried

3/4 cup Sour-Cream Substitute, page 241

1/4 teaspoon garlic powder

2 tablespoons minced chives

1/4 teaspoon dill weed

Leaf lettuce

Dash of paprika or to taste

Cut an *X* across top of each tomato and down sides, being careful not to cut through to the bottom. Scoop out half of pulp from each tomato, save for use in another dish. Set tomatoes cut-side down on paper towel to drain. In a small bowl, combine Sour-Cream Substitute, garlic powder, chives and dill weed. With a small spoon, carefully stuff tomatoes with herb mixture. Arrange on a platter lined with leaf lettuce and sprinkle with paprika. Refrigerate 4 to 6 hours until ready to serve.

Yield: 25 servings

1 serving contains:

Cal	Prot	Fat	Chol	Carb	Fib	Sodium
9kc	1gm	trace	trace	1gm	trace	30mg

Fresh-Fruit Kabobs

*Terrific served with Fresh-Fruit Dip,
page 32*

**1 fresh pineapple, cubed, about 2
cups**

**2 cups fresh strawberries, washed,
dried, not hulled**

3 oranges, peeled, sectioned

Leaf lettuce

Mint sprigs to garnish

Divide fruit among 10 wooden skewers,
alternating different fruits. Refrigerate 2
hours until serving time. To serve, arrange on a platter lined with leaf lettuce.
Garnish with mint sprigs.

Yield: 10 servings

1 serving contains:

Cal	Prot	Fat	Chol	Carb	Fib	Sodium
45kc	1gm	trace	0	11gm	2gm	1mg

Quesadillas

Quick and easy appetizer or great with a green salad for a weekend supper.

4 large flour tortillas

1 cup (4 oz.) shredded low-fat cheddar cheese

2 oz. green chiles

Heat a large non-stick skillet over medium heat; add a tortilla and heat briefly. Sprinkle with 1/2 cup cheese and about half the chilies, top with another tortilla. Heat until cheese is melted, pressing together lightly. Repeat with remaining tortillas. To serve, cut in half or in quarters.

Yield: 4 servings (1/2 quesadilla each)

1 serving contains:

Cal	Prot	Fat	Chol	Carb	Fib	Sodium
178kc	11gm	6gm	20mg	19gm	0	210mg

Soups

Homemade soups are a wonderful source of good nutrition—when a wise choice of ingredients, vitamins, fiber and minerals fill the soup pot. Soups in this section have been chosen because they are low in fat and cholesterol and high in taste appeal.

You can make a broth almost fat-free by chilling it and removing the layer of solid fat that conveniently rises to the surface. You can add nutrition by saving the water from cooking vegetables and freezing it to boost a soup at a later date. You can also add leftover vegetables to soups. Substitute herbs and spices for that extra dash of salt, and you will increase the flavor and decrease the sodium. To add a little body to a soup, use whole grains and egg-yolk-free pastas.

Use your imagination—be creative. Make a pot of soup from scratch and enjoy it for lunch or as the main dish for dinner with a salad and some home-baked or bakery bread. Make a large pot and freeze the extra to use later. You can always stretch soup with leftovers that might not be enough for a complete meal.

Hints for Preparing Dried Beans

Beans can bring variety and extra nutrition to your menu for such a small price. They are high in protein, magnesium, vitamins and fiber, low in fat and easy to store.

Most dried beans should be soaked overnight to restore the water lost in drying and this will also shorten the cooking time. When soaking beans, use a large container to allow for expansion of the beans. Use at least 6 cups of water for each pound of dried beans.

If you forget to presoak the beans, place them in boiling water and boil for 3 minutes, then let them stand, covered, for 1 to 2 hours. Rinse and proceed with your recipe.

If you have a problem with beans "talking back" to you, try the following hint: Discard the soak water, cover the beans with fresh water and cook for 30 minutes. Discard that water, add more fresh water and a pinch of ginger, then proceed to cook until beans are tender.

One pound of dried beans equals 2 cups in volume. Dried beans double in weight and volume when cooked so 2 cups dried beans will give you 4 cups cooked beans.

For tender beans, cook over a low heat and do not add salt until the beans are almost cooked. If the beans appear to be drying out, add more water during cooking.

Chilled Rhubarb Soup

Serve this colorful soup before or after dinner.

2 cups cubed rhubarb, fresh or frozen

1 tablespoon cornstarch

2 cups water

1/4 cup plus 1 tablespoon sugar

1/8 teaspoon ground cinnamon

1/8 teaspoon ground allspice

2 tablespoons Marsala wine

4 teaspoons plain low-fat yogurt

Variation

Chilled Blueberry Soup: Substitute 2 cups fresh or frozen blueberries for rhubarb; reduce sugar to 3 tablespoons.

Place rhubarb in a medium-size saucepan. In a small bowl, blend cornstarch and water; add to rhubarb. Cover and bring rhubarb to a boil over medium heat; reduce heat to low and cook 10 minutes or until tender. Add sugar, cinnamon, allspice and wine. Pour into a blender or food processor fitted with the metal blade; process about 20 seconds or until smooth. Refrigerate 2 to 8 hours until ready to serve. To serve, pour soup into 4 individual bowls. Top soup in each bowl with 1 teaspoon yogurt; gently swirl yogurt to make an attractive design.

Yield: 4 (1/2-cup) servings

1 serving contains:

Cal	Prot	Fat	Chol	Carb	Fib	Sodium
90kc	1gm	trace	trace	21gm	0	7mg

Chilled Cherry Soup

Great on a hot summer day.

1 (1-lb.) can red sour cherries, pitted

2 teaspoons cornstarch

1/4 cup sugar

1/8 teaspoon ground cinnamon

1-1/2 teaspoons finely grated orange peel

1/2 cup orange juice

2 tablespoons Marsala wine

4 teaspoons Sour-Cream Substitute, page 241

Pour cherries and juice into a blender or food processor fitted with the metal blade; process about 20 seconds or until smooth to make cherry purée. Pour into a medium-size saucepan; set aside. In a small bowl, combine cornstarch, sugar and cinnamon. Stir in a little cherry purée. When blended, stir in remaining cherry purée. Add 1 teaspoon orange peel and juice. Bring to a boil over medium heat; reduce heat to low and cook about 2 minutes, stirring constantly. Stir in wine. Refrigerate 2 to 8 hours until ready to serve. To serve, pour soup into 4 individual bowls. Top soup in each bowl with 1 teaspoon Sour-Cream Substitute and sprinkle with remaining orange peel.

Yield: 4 (1/2-cup) servings

1 serving contains:

Cal	Prot	Fat	Chol	Carb	Fib	Sodium
132kc	4gm	trace	1mg	29gm	trace	87mg

Black-eyed-Pea Soup

Plays an important role in our New Year's dinner because—according to Southern tradition—black-eyed peas bring good luck.

1 lb. black-eyed peas

6 cups water

1/2 cup minced onion

1 bay leaf

1 teaspoon salt

Dash of red-pepper sauce or to taste

1 tablespoon low-fat margarine

2 beef bouillon cubes

1 garlic clove, crushed

The night before, sort and wash peas; put in a large kettle. Add water to cover and soak overnight in a cool place. The next morning, discard soak water and add 6 cups fresh water to cover. Add remaining ingredients and cook over low heat 2 hours or until beans are tender. Serve immediately.

Yield: 16 (1/2-cup) servings

1 serving contains:

Cal	Prot	Fat	Chol	Carb	Fib	Sodium
29kc	2gm	1gm	0	4gm	trace	240mg

Chicken-Corn Chowder

Begs for a tossed green salad to accompany it.

1-1/2 chicken breasts, skinned

1 bay leaf

3/4 teaspoon dried-leaf thyme

1/2 teaspoon salt

1/8 teaspoon dried-leaf marjoram

2 garlic cloves, minced

1 tablespoon parsley flakes

1/4 teaspoon pepper

3 quarts water

2 chicken bouillon cubes

1 cup chopped celery

1 cup chopped onion

1 cup chopped carrot

2 cups whole-kernel corn, fresh or frozen

2 cups Baking Mix, page 65

2/3 cup water

In a soup kettle, combine chicken, bay leaf, thyme, salt, marjoram, garlic, parsley, pepper and water. Cover, bring to a boil over high heat. Reduce heat to mediuim-low and cook about 45 minutes. Add bouillon cubes, celery and onion; cook about 15 minutes longer or until chicken is tender. Remove chicken from broth; cool. Remove and discard bone from chicken. Chop chicken into medium-size chunks; set aside. Add carrot to broth and cook until almost tender, adding corn during final few minutes. Adjust heat to get a gentle boil. In a medium-size bowl, combine Baking Mix and 2/3 cup water; stir with a fork until it forms a soft dough. Drop by the teaspoon into boiling kettle of vegetables. Cook, uncovered, over a low heat 10 minutes, then cover and cook about 10 minutes longer. Add chicken and heat through. Serve immediately.

Yield: 14 (1-cup) servings

1 serving contains:

Cal	Prot	Fat	Chol	Carb	Fib	Sodium
116kc	8gm	2gm	16mg	16gm	1gm	467mg

New England-Style Clam Chowder

A family favorite, now with less fat.

1/2 cup chopped onion

1/2 cup chopped celery

2 cups chicken broth

2 cups diced potatoes

2 cups clam nectar

1/4 teaspoon lemon pepper

1/8 teaspoon freshly ground black pepper

1/8 teaspoon garlic powder

1/2 tablespoon parsley flakes

2-1/2 cups skim milk

2 tablespoons non-fat powdered milk

5 tablespoons all-purpose flour

3 tablespoons cornstarch

2 cups minced clams, fresh or canned

In a large soup kettle over medium heat, cook onion and celery in 1 tablespoon chicken broth until tender. Add remaining chicken broth and potatoes; cook until tender. Add clam nectar, lemon pepper, black pepper, garlic powder and parsley; bring to a gentle boil. In a quart jar with a lid, combine 2-1/2 cups skim milk, powdered milk, flour and cornstarch; shake until smooth. Slowly add to soup, stirring constantly, until it starts to thicken. Add clams and heat through; do not boil. Serve immediately.

Yield: 8 (1-cup) servings

1 serving contains:

Cal	Prot	Fat	Chol	Carb	Fib	Sodium
168kc	13gm	2gm	59mg	24gm	1gm	296mg

Chicken Gumbo

Makes a light, nutritious lunch.

1/2 cup chopped onion

1/2 cup chopped celery

4 cups chicken broth

2 cups stewed tomatoes

1/4 cup uncooked long-grain white rice

1/2 cup chopped green bell pepper

1 cup sliced okra

1 bay leaf

1/4 teaspoon salt

Pepper to taste

1 cup chopped cooked chicken breast

In a large soup kettle over medium heat, cook onion and celery in 1 tablespoon broth until tender. Add remaining chicken broth, tomatoes and rice; bring to a boil. Reduce heat to low and cook 10 minutes. Add green pepper, okra, bay leaf, salt and pepper; cook about 45 minutes or until vegetables are tender. Add chicken and heat through. Serve immediately.

Yield: 10 (1-cup) servings

1 serving contains:

Cal	Prot	Fat	Chol	Carb	Fib	Sodium
85 kc	9gm	1gm	15mg	10gm	1gm	508mg

Chicken-Vegetable Soup with Herb Dumplings

Dumplings make this a complete meal.

1-1/2 chicken breasts, skinned

1 bay leaf

1/2 teaspoon salt

3 quarts water

2 chicken bouillon cubes

1 cup diced celery

1/2 cup diced onion

3 cups frozen mixed vegetables

1 cup diced potato

2 cups Baking Mix, page 65

1 teaspoon minced fresh parsley

1 teaspoon snipped chives

1/2 teaspoon dried-leaf thyme

1/8 teaspoon white pepper

2/3 cup water

In a soup kettle, combine chicken, bay leaf, salt and water; bring to a boil. Reduce heat and simmer about 45 minutes. Add bouillon cubes, celery and onion. Cook about 15 minutes or until chicken is tender. Remove chicken from broth; cool. Remove and discard bone from chicken. Chop chicken into chunks; set aside. Add mixed vegetables and cook about 5 minutes. Add potato and cook about 15 minutes longer or until all vegetables are tender. In a bowl, combine Baking Mix, parsley, chives, thyme and pepper. Add water and stir with a fork until it forms a soft dough. Bring soup to a boil. Drop dough by the teaspoon into gently boiling soup. Reduce heat to low. Cook, uncovered, 10 minutes, then cover and cook 10 minutes longer. Add chicken, heat through. Serve immediately.

Yield: 14 (1-cup) servings

1 serving contains:

Cal	Prot	Fat	Chol	Carb	Fib	Sodium
123kc	9gm	2gm	16mg	16gm	2gm	472mg

Clam-Corn Chowder

A unique blending of flavors.

1 cup chopped onion

1 cup chopped celery

1/2 cup water

2 tomatoes, peeled, chopped, about 1-1/2 cups

2 tablespoons minced fresh parsley

2 cups cubed potatoes

1 teaspoon low-fat margarine

4 oz. fresh mushrooms, thinly sliced

2 (10-1/2-oz.) cans cream of mushroom soup or 2 recipes Basic White Sauce with mushrooms, page 236

4 cups skim milk

2 cups whole-kernel corn

1/2 teaspoon lemon pepper

1/4 teaspoon black pepper

2 (6-1/2-oz.) cans minced clams, or 4 quarts unshucked fresh clams

In a large soup kettle over medium heat, cook onion and celery in water until tender. Add tomatoes, parsley and potatoes; cook until tender. In a small non-stick skillet, heat margarine; add mushrooms and cook 5 minutes. While mushrooms are cooking, stir soup or sauce, milk, corn and peppers into vegetables in kettle. Reduce heat to medium-low and simmer 10 minutes. Add clams and mushrooms; simmer 5 minutes longer. Serve immediately.

Yield: 12 (1-cup) servings

1 serving contains:

Cal	Prot	Fat	Chol	Carb	Fib	Sodium
164kc	8gm	5gm	21mg	24gm	2gm	496mg

Hearty Chicken-Noodle Soup

So hearty, you'll be tempted to eat it with a fork.

1-1/2 chicken breasts, skinned

3 quarts water

2 chicken bouillon cubes

1 garlic clove, minced

1 bay leaf

3/4 teaspoon dried-leaf thyme

1 tablespoon minced fresh parsley

1 teaspoon salt

1/4 teaspoon pepper

3 cups sliced carrot

2 cups sliced celery

1 cup chopped onion

8 oz. noodles, yolk-free if available

In a large soup kettle, place chicken, water, bouillon cubes, garlic, bay leaf, thyme, parsley, salt and pepper. Cover and bring to a boil over high heat. Reduce heat to low and simmer 45 to 50 minutes or until chicken is tender. Remove chicken to a plate; cool. Remove and discard bone from chicken. Cut chicken into chunks; set aside. Add carrot, celery and onion to broth; simmer about 30 minutes or until almost tender. Add noodles and cook according to package directions. Add chicken during final few minutes to heat through. Serve immediately.

Yield: 12 (1-cup) servings

1 serving contains:

Cal	Prot	Fat	Chol	Carb	Fib	Sodium
111kc	9gm	1gm	30mg.	15gm	2gm	416mg

Joyce's Cream of Broccoli Soup

A delicate cream soup, that's low in fat.

1 large bunch of broccoli, about 6 cups chopped

3-1/2 cups chicken broth

1/4 cup chopped onion

1/4 cup chopped celery

1/4 cup all-purpose flour

2 cups skim milk

1/4 teaspoon imitation butter flavoring

1/2 teaspoon salt

Pepper to taste

Ground nutmeg to taste

Rinse and chop broccoli, cutting through stems for faster cooking. In a soup kettle over medium heat, simmer broccoli in chicken broth until tender. Using a slotted spoon, lift broccoli out of broth. Reserve several broccoli flowerets for garnish. Put remaining broccoli, onion and celery in a blender or a food processor fitted with the metal blade; process until smooth, then set aside. In a jar with a lid, combine flour and milk; shake until dissolved. Slowly add to chicken broth, stirring until it starts to thicken slightly. Add puréed broccoli mixture, butter flavoring, salt, pepper and nutmeg, stirring just until soup starts to simmer; do not boil. Garnish with reserved broccoli flowerets before serving.

Yield: 6 (1-cup) servings

1 serving contains:

Cal	Prot	Fat	Chol	Carb	Fib	Sodium
96 kc	9gm	1gm	2mg	14gm	3gm	686mg

Lentil Soup

A tasty, economical dish.

1-1/3 cups dried lentils

1 cup chopped onion

1 cup chopped celery

1/2 cup water

1 bay leaf

3 beef bouillon cubes

1 teaspoon salt

1/4 teaspoon pepper

1/2 cup tomato sauce

1 tablespoon red-wine vinegar

1/2 teaspoon Italian seasoning

Sort and wash lentils. Place in a large container; add cold water to cover and let soak about 3 hours. Pour into a colander to drain. In a large soup kettle over medium-low heat, cook onion and celery in 1/2 cup water until tender. Add lentils and enough water to cover them well; bring to a boil. Add bay leaf and bouillon cubes; reduce heat and simmer about 1 hour. Add salt, pepper, tomato sauce, vinegar and Italian seasoning; simmer about 30 minutes or until tender. Serve immediately.

Yield: 8 (1-cup) servings

1 serving contains:

Cal	Prot	Fat	Chol	Carb	Fib	Sodium
87 kc	6gm	trace	0	16gm	4gm	695mg

Minestrone

A complete, nutritious meal in one pot.

1-1/2 cups dried beans, navy or
  pintos

6 cups water

3 beef bouillon cubes

1-1/2 quarts water

4-1/2 cups stewed tomatoes

1/2 cup tomato sauce

1/3 cup uncooked brown rice or
  elbow macaroni

1-1/2 cups chopped celery

2 cups sliced carrot

1 cup chopped onion

2 garlic cloves, minced

2 tablespoons chopped fresh parsley

1/2 teaspoon dried-leaf thyme

1/2 teaspoon dried-leaf oregano

2 cups chopped cabbage

1 cup cubed zucchini

Sort and wash beans. Place in a large kettle; add cold water to cover and soak overnight. Next day, rinse beans and return to large kettle; add 6 cups water. Bring to a boil over high heat; reduce heat and simmer until tender. Add bouillon cubes. Put 1-1/2 quarts water, tomatoes and tomato sauce in a large kettle; bring to a boil. Add rice and reduce heat; simmer about 15 minutes. Add celery, carrot, onion, garlic, parsley, thyme and oregano; simmer about 20 minutes. Add cabbage and zucchini; cook about 15 minutes or until all vegetables are tender. Add cooked beans and liquid; heat through. Serve immediately.

Yield: 12 (1-cup) servings

1 serving contains:

Cal	Prot	Fat	Chol	Carb	Fib	Sodium
118kc	6gm	1gm	0	24gm	5gm	558mg

Onion Soup

Combine with a sandwich for a great meal.

2 quarts chicken broth

7 cups sliced sweet onions, about 4 medium-size onions

2 garlic cloves, minced

1/4 teaspoon ground nutmeg

2 teaspoons Worcestershire sauce

2 teaspoons all-purpose flour

1/4 cup water

4 slices French bread, cut in half

1/2 cup shredded part-skim-milk mozzarella cheese

Put broth in a large soup kettle; add onions. Bring to a boil; reduce heat and simmer about 1-1/2 hours. Add garlic, nutmeg and Worcestershire sauce; simmer 10 minutes. In a small jar with a lid, combine flour and water; shake until completely dissolved. Stirring constantly, slowly add flour mixture to soup; simmer 5 minutes longer. To serve, preheat broiler. Place 1/2 slice of bread in the bottom of 8 individual ovenproof soup bowls. Carefully ladle soup into bowls. Sprinkle each serving with 1 tablespoon cheese. Place under broiler until cheese is melted and starting to brown. Serve immediately.

Yield: 8 (1-cup) servings

1 serving contains:

Cal	Prot	Fat	Chol	Carb	Fib	Sodium
161kc	10gm	4gm	5mg	22gm	3gm	921mg

Potato-Leek Soup

Leek adds a distinctive taste to this creamy soup.

2 cups sliced leek, white part only

1 cup chopped onion

1/2 cup water

3 cups diced potato

8 cups chicken broth

1/8 teaspoon black pepper

1/2 teaspoon dried-leaf marjoram

2 tablespoons all-purpose flour

2 tablespoons cornstarch

2 tablespoons non-fat powdered milk

1 cup skimmed evaporated milk

1 cup skim milk

Snipped chives to garnish

In a large soup kettle over medium-high heat, cook leek and onion in 1/2 cup water until tender. Add potato, chicken broth, pepper and marjoram; bring to a boil. Reduce heat and simmer about 1-1/2 hours. Put leek, onion and potato in a blender or a food processor fitted with the metal blade; process until smooth. Return to kettle over low heat. In a jar with a lid, combine flour, cornstarch, powdered milk, evaporated milk and skim milk; shake until completely dissolved. Slowly pour into vegetable mixture, stirring constantly; continue to stir often until soup starts to thicken. Serve immediately or refrigerate and serve chilled. Garnish with snipped chives to serve.

Yield: 11 (1-cup) servings

1 serving contains:

Cal	Prot	Fat	Chol	Carb	Fib	Sodium
153kc	8gm	1gm	2mg	27gm	2gm	619mg

Breads

With the emphasis on good nutrition and fiber in today's diet, whole grains are recognized as a popular ingredient in our diets. I have included Banana Bread, Oat-Bran Muffins and Honey Whole-Wheat Bread because of their extra nutritional value and enjoyable taste. But I also enjoy other breads made with unbleached flour, such as Biscuits, Jean's Italian Bread or Corn Bread. You may use all-purpose flour rather than the unbleached I prefer. These foods contain similar levels of protein, complex carbohydrates, vitamins and minerals and are certainly not "junk food." So as long as a bread conforms to your diet—enjoy!

Hints For Making Bread: When making bread, strong beating of the dough is a must. This can be accomplished either with the dough hook of a heavy-duty electric mixer or by hand using a large spoon. Kneading also can be done either by a heavy-duty mixer or by hand on a lightly floured counter top. Test the dough by making an indentation with your finger; if the dough springs back, it has been kneaded enough. Put the dough in a warm, lightly greased bowl, cover with a cloth and set in a draft-free place to rise. When the dough has doubled in size, press your finger lightly into the dough. If an indentation remains, the dough is ready to shape. Turn out dough onto a lightly floured surface. Knead a minute or two, shape, put into lightly greased pans and set aside, in a draft-free place, covered with a cloth. When dough has again doubled in size, touch lightly with one finger; if it feels light and springy it is ready to bake. Bake according to the individual recipe. When bread appears done, tap the top of the loaf with your knuckle. It should sound hollow. Turn out the bread to cool on a rack. When cool, wrap and secure well to store. All breads freeze well but should be securely wrapped in two plastic bags.

When making muffins, I prefer to use foil muffin-tin liners. If these are not available, lightly spray the muffin tin with vegetable spray. I have found when I use paper liners, the bottom portion of the muffin sticks to the paper. I always bake Corn Bread in an iron skillet because it makes a crisp crust.

Baking Mix

Don't be caught without some in the refrigerator.

9 cups unbleached or all-purpose flour, sifted

1/3 cup baking powder

1 cup non-fat powdered milk

1 tablespoon salt

1-3/4 cups low-fat margarine

In a large bowl, combine flour, baking powder, powdered milk and salt. With a pastry blender or two knives, cut margarine into mixture until the texture of cornmeal. Store in tightly sealed containers in the refrigerator.

Yield: 60 (1/4-cup) servings or 15 cups

Will keep 2 to 3 months refrigerated.

1 serving contains:

Cal	Prot	Fat	Chol	Carb	Fib	Sodium
92kc	2gm	3gm	trace	14gm	trace	258mg

Homemade Biscuits

Use your imagination and experiment.

2 cups Baking Mix, page 65

1/2 cup water

Preheat oven to 425F (220C). In a medium-size bowl, combine Baking Mix and water with a fork, stirring until moistened. Turn out on a floured board and knead about 15 times. Roll out to 1/2-inch thick. Cut out biscuits with a round cutter. Place on an ungreased baking sheet. Bake 10 minutes or until lightly browned.

Yield: 5 servings (2 biscuits each)

1 serving contains:

Cal	Prot	Fat	Chol	Carb	Fib	Sodium
154kc	4gm	4gm	trace	24gm	1gm	399mg

Variation:

Cheesy Biscuits: Before mixing ingredients, add 1/3 cup low-fat shredded cheese.

Herb Biscuits: Before mixing ingredients, add your favorite herbs. Mix flavors to enhance your entree.

Italian—1/2 teaspoon crushed dried leaf Italian herbs
Peppy—1/4 teaspoon dry mustard and 1/2 teaspoon ground sage
Chives—1/4 cup minced chives
Dill—1 tablespoon dried dill
Parsley—1 tablespoon chopped fresh parsley
Onion—1/4 cup minced onions

Blueberry Muffins

For additional fiber substitute 1/3 cup
oat bran for 1/3 cup flour.

1-1/3 cups unbleached or
   all-purpose flour

1 cup oats, quick or regular,
   uncooked

1/4 cup firmly packed brown sugar

1 tablespoon baking powder

1/2 teaspoon ground cinnamon

1 cup skim milk

2 egg whites, slightly beaten

2 tablespoons oil of choice

1 cup fresh or frozen blueberries

Preheat oven to 400F (205C). Line a
12-cup muffin pan with foil liners or
spray a non-stick pan with vegetable
spray. In a large bowl, combine flour,
oats, sugar, baking powder and cinnamon. Add milk, egg whites and oil; stir
until blended. Lightly fold in blueberries. Spoon into muffin cups, filling
about 2/3 full. Bake 25 to 30 minutes or
until lightly browned. Cool about 5 minutes before serving.

Yields: 12 servings (1 muffin each)

1 serving contains:

Cal	Prot	Fat	Chol	Carb	Fib	Sodium
132kc	4gm	3gm	trace	23gm	1gm	106mg

Oat-Bran Muffins

*Begin your day with a bran muffin and
a bowl of fresh fruit.*

**1-1/2 cups unbleached or
   all-purpose flour**

1 cup oat bran

3 teaspoons baking powder

2 egg whites, slightly beaten

3/4 cup skim milk

1/4 cup molasses

3 tablespoons oil of choice

Preheat oven to 400F (205C). Line a
12-cup muffin pan with foil liners or
spray a non-stick pan with vegetable
spray. In a medium-size bowl, combine
flour, bran and baking powder. In a
small bowl, combine egg whites, milk,
molasses and oil. Add to dry ingredients; stir just until well-blended. Spoon
into muffin cups, filling about 2/3 full.
Bake 20 minutes or until lightly
browned. Cool about 5 minutes before
serving.

Yield: 12 servings (1 muffin each)

1 serving contains:

Cal	Prot	Fat	Chol	Carb	Fib	Sodium
134kc	4gm	4gm	trace	21gm	2gm	109mg

Variation:

Add 1 cup raisins or finely chopped
   apple or dates and 1 teaspoon ground
   cinnamon.

Cornmeal Muffins

Use fresh corn for a wonderful summer treat.

1 cup cornmeal

3/4 cup unbleached or all-purpose flour

3 tablespoons sugar

3 teaspoons baking powder

1/2 teaspoon salt

2 egg whites, slightly beaten

2/3 cup skim milk

1 cup creamed corn

Preheat oven to 425F (220C). Line a 12-cup muffin pan with foil liners or spray a non-stick pan with vegetable spray. In a large bowl, combine all dry ingredients. Add remaining ingredients and stir until well-blended. Spoon into muffin cups, filling about 2/3 full. Bake 20 minutes or until lightly browned. Cool about 5 minutes before removing.

Yield: 12 servings (1 muffin each)

1 serving contains:

Cal	Prot	Fat	Chol	Carb	Fib	Sodium
106kc	3gm	trace	trace	23gm	trace	243mg

Oatmeal Muffins

Try using chopped prunes, dates or apricots instead of raisins.

2 cups unbleached or all-purpose flour

1/2 cup sugar

2 tablespoons baking powder

1/2 teaspoon salt

1 teaspoon ground cinnamon

2 cups oats, quick or regular, uncooked

1/4 cup oil of choice

3 egg whites, slightly beaten

2 cups skim milk

1 cup raisins

Preheat oven to 400F (205C). Line 18 muffin cups with foil liners or spray non-stick pans with vegetable spray. In a large bowl, combine flour, sugar, baking powder, salt, cinnamon and oats. In a small bowl, combine oil, egg whites and milk. Pour over dry ingredients all at one time; stir until mixed. Fold in raisins. Do not over-mix. Spoon batter into muffin cups, filling 2/3 full. Bake 20 minutes or until lightly browned. Cool about 5 minutes before serving.

Yield: 18 large muffins

1 serving contains:

Cal	Prot	Fat	Chol	Carb	Fib	Sodium
170kc	5gm	4gm	trace	30gm	1gm	191mg

Banana-Raisin Bread

A traditional bread with the added goodness of whole wheat and oat bran.

1/3 cup oil of choice

1 cup firmly packed brown sugar

3 ripe bananas, mashed

1 teaspoon vanilla extract

3 egg whites, slightly beaten

1-1/2 cups whole-wheat flour

1/2 cup oat bran or wheat germ

2 teaspoons baking powder

1/2 teaspoon ground cinnamon

1/2 cup raisins

Variation:

Substitute 1 cup all-purpose flour for 1 cup whole-wheat flour. Reduce sugar to 1/2 cup.

Preheat oven to 325F (165C). Spray a 9" x 5" loaf pan with vegetable spray. In a large bowl, combine oil and sugar. Add bananas, vanilla and egg whites; set aside. In a medium-size bowl, combine flour, oat bran or wheat germ, baking powder and cinnamon. Add to banana mixture; stir until combined. Stir in raisins. Pour into prepared pan. Bake 1 hour 10 minutes or until a wooden pick comes out clean. Turn out on a rack to cool. This makes a dense loaf.

Yield: 10 servings (1 slice each)

1 serving contains:

Cal	Prot	Fat	Chol	Carb	Fib	Sodium
284kc	5gm	8gm	0	52gm	5gm	92mg

Corn Bread

Corn bread and beans is our daughter's favorite meal.

1 cup cornmeal

1 cup unbleached or all-purpose flour

5 teaspoons baking powder

1/2 teaspoon salt

1 cup skim milk

2 egg whites, slightly beaten

1 teaspoon oil of choice

Variation

For a sweeter bread, add 1/4 cup sugar.

Preheat oven to 425F (220C). Combine cornmeal, flour, baking powder and salt in a medium-size bowl. Add milk and egg whites; stir well. Heat a 9-inch iron skillet or ovenproof pan over medium-high heat. Add oil; while this is heating, mix batter. Pour batter into hot skillet. Bake 20 minutes or until golden brown. Serve warm.

Yield: 8 (3-1/2-inch) wedges

1 serving contains:

Cal	Prot	Fat	Chol	Carb	Fib	Sodium
142kc	5gm	1gm	1mg	28gm	trace	363mg

Lemon Bread

Serve with iced tea for a refreshing summer dessert or snack.

1/2 cup low-fat margarine

1-1/4 cups sugar

1/4 cup egg substitute (equivalent of 1 egg)

2 egg whites

1-1/4 cups unbleached or all-purpose flour, sifted

1-1/2 teaspoons baking powder

1/4 teaspoon salt

1/2 cup skim milk

3 teaspoons grated lemon peel

3 tablespoons fresh lemon juice

Preheat oven to 350F (175C). Spray a 9" x 5" loaf pan with vegetable spray. In a large bowl, beat margarine and 1 cup sugar until light and fluffy. In a small bowl, beat egg substitute and egg whites together. Add to sugar mixture. Sift flour, baking powder and salt into a medium-size bowl. Add to sugar mixture, alternating dry ingredients with milk; mix well. Stir in lemon peel. Pour into pan. Bake 1 hour or until a wooden pick comes out clean. In a small bowl, combine 1/4 cup sugar and lemon juice; stir until sugar is dissolved. Drizzle over warm bread while still in pan. Let stand 5 minutes, then invert onto a cake rack; remove pan and turn bread right side up. Let cool before slicing.

Yield: 10 servings (1 slice each)

1 serving contains:

Cal	Prot	Fat	Chol	Carb	Fib	Sodium
197kc	3gm	5gm	trace	36gm	trace	238mg

Mexican Corn Bread

Great served with a hearty bean soup or chili.

1/4 cup diced green chilies, drained

1 cup unbleached or all-purpose flour

1 cup plus 1 teaspoon cornmeal

4 teaspoons baking powder

1/2 teaspoon salt

1 tablespoon sugar

2 egg whites, slightly beaten

2/3 cup milk

1 cup creamed corn

1 teaspoon oil of choice

Preheat oven to 425F (220C). Lay green chilies on paper towels to drain. In a large bowl, combine flour, 1 cup cornmeal, baking powder, salt and sugar. Add egg whites and milk; stir. Add corn and chilies; stir. Batter should be thin enough to pour into skillet, but not runny. Add more milk if needed for pouring consistency. Heat oil in a 9-inch iron skillet or ovenproof pan. Sprinkle 1 teaspoon cornmeal into hot skillet and heat just a few seconds until cornmeal is lightly browned. Pour batter into skillet. Bake 30 minutes or until lightly browned. Invert onto a round 10-inch heatproof serving plate. Serve warm.

Yield: 8 (3-1/2-inch) wedges

1 serving contains:

Cal	Prot	Fat	Chol	Carb	Fib	Sodium
123kc	4gm	1gm	trace	25gm	trace	439mg

Whole-wheat Molasses Bread

Great for luncheon sandwiches.

Cornmeal, if desired

1/2 cup molasses

1 cup skim milk

1/4 cup unbleached or all-purpose flour

2 cups whole-wheat flour

1/2 cup sugar

1 teaspoon baking soda

1/4 teaspoon salt

Preheat oven to 350F (175C). Lightly oil a 9" x 5" loaf pan or spray with vegetable spray; sprinkle with cornmeal, if desired. In a medium-size bowl, combine molasses and milk. In another medium-size bowl, combine flours, sugar, baking soda and salt. Add to molasses and milk; stir until well-mixed. Pour into loaf pan. Bake 1 hour or until a wooden pick comes out clean. Invert onto a rack and cool.

Yield: 10 slices (1 slice per serving)

1 serving contains:

Cal	Prot	Fat	Chol	Carb	Fib	Sodium
172kc	4gm	trace	trace	39gm	3gm	159mg

Dilly Bread

Dill gives it that tantalizing flavor.

**1 (1/4-oz.) pkg. dry yeast, about
     1 tablespoon**

1/4 cup warm water (110F, 45C)

**1 cup low-fat small-curd cottage
     cheese, room temperature**

2 tablespoons sugar

2 tablespoons minced onion

1 tablespoon low-fat margarine

2 teaspoons dill weed

1 teaspoon salt

1/4 teaspoon baking soda

2 egg whites, slightly beaten

**2-1/2 cups unbleached or
     all-purpose flour**

1 teaspoon cornmeal

In a small bowl, dissolve yeast in water; set aside. In a large bowl, combine cottage cheese, sugar, onion, margarine, dill, salt and baking soda. Add egg whites to yeast mixture; mix well. Add to cottage-cheese mixture, blending well. If you have a mixer with a dough hook, use it. If not, mix and knead by hand on a floured board. Gradually add flour and beat until dough pulls away from bowl, about 5 minutes, or knead by hand on a floured board. Place in a greased bowl. Cover and let rise in a warm place until doubled in bulk. Preheat oven to 350F (175C). Spray a shallow round 2-quart casserole with vegetable spray; dust with cornmeal. When dough has doubled, punch down and knead again a few times. Put in prepared casserole. Let rise again until doubled. Bake 40 to 50 minutes or until lightly browned. Remove from pan. Cool before slicing.

Yield: 12 servings (1 slice each)

1 serving contains:

Cal	Prot	Fat	Chol	Carb	Fib	Sodium
126kc	6gm	1gm	1mg	23gm	1gm	277mg

Honey Whole-wheat Bread

My own blue-ribbon recipe.

2 cups whole-wheat flour

5 to 6 cups unbleached or all-purpose flour

1 cup non-fat powdered milk

3 (1/4 oz.) pkgs. active dry yeast, about 3 tablespoons

1 tablespoon salt

2 cups warm water (110F, 45C)

1/3 cup oil of choice

1/3 cup honey

Cornmeal, if desired

In a bowl, combine 2 cups flour, dry milk, yeast and salt. Add all liquids and mix well. Stir in 4 cups flour. If you have a dough hook, use it. If not, mix and knead by hand. Add remaining flour, 1/2 cup at a time, until dough clings to hook and cleans side of bowl. Knead 7 to 10 minutes, until smooth and elastic. Add flour if necessary to keep sides of bowl clean. Make an indentation with your finger in dough; it will spring back if it is kneaded enough. Place in a lightly oiled bowl. Cover with a cloth and let rise until double. Press your finger lightly into dough. If indentation remains, dough is ready. Lightly oil three (9" x 5") loaf pans; sprinkle with cornmeal, if desired. Punch dough down and turn out onto a lightly floured board; knead 1 or 2 minutes. Divide and shape into loaves. Place in prepared pans; cover with a cloth. Let rise until double. Preheat oven to 375F (190C). Bake 20 to 25 minutes or until golden brown. Cool before slicing.

Yield: 15 servings (2 slices each)

1 serving contains:

Cal	Prot	Fat	Chol	Carb	Fib	Sodium
306kc	9gm	5gm	1mg	55gm	3gm	418mg

Jean's Italian Bread

For added flavor, sprinkle with 3 to 4 tablespoons chopped herbs after dough is rolled into a rectangle.

2 (1/4-oz.) pkg. active dry yeast, about 2 tablespoons

1 tablespoon salt

1 tablespoon sugar

5 to 6 cups unbleached or all-purpose flour

2 cups warm water (110F, 45C)

1 tablespoon low-fat margarine, melted

Lightly oil a large bowl. In another bowl, combine yeast, salt, sugar and 2 cups flour; stir to blend. Add water and mix. Stir in 2 more cups flour. Put in mixer with a dough hook. If kneading by hand, knead until smooth and elastic. Gradually add remaining flour, 1/2 cup at a time as needed. Mix until dough clings to hook and cleans sides of bowl. Continue kneading 5 minutes. Place dough in prepared bowl. Make a slight indentation on top and pour margarine over top. Spread over all. Cover and let rise until doubled. Spray a cookie sheet with vegetable spray. On a floured surface, punch down dough and divide into two equal parts. Roll each half into a rectangle, then roll up jelly-roll fashion. Place on prepared cookie sheet, seam side down. Set in a cold oven 30 minutes. Leaving bread in oven, set oven to 400F (205C) and bake 30 minutes or until lightly browned. Cool before slicing.

Yield: 15 servings (2 slices per serving) or 2 loaves

1 serving (2 slices each) contains:

Cal	Prot	Fat	Chol	Carb	Fib	Sodium
176kc	5gm	1gm	0	36gm	1gm	401mg

Hot Garlic Bread

Great accompaniment for your favorite Italian dish.

3 tablespoons low-fat margarine, room flavor

1/2 teaspoon parsley flakes

1/8 teaspoon ground oregano

1/8 teaspoon dill weed

1/8 teaspoon garlic powder

1 (1-lb.) loaf Italian bread

1 tablespoon grated Parmesan cheese

Preheat oven to 400F (205C). In a small bowl, blend margarine, parsley, oregano, dill and garlic powder. Slice bread and spread herb mixture on one side of each slice. Reassemble slices forming a loaf. Place on a large sheet of aluminum foil. Fold foil over sides, leaving top open (shape like a boat). Sprinkle Parmesan cheese over bread. Bake 10 minutes or until lightly browned. Serve hot.

Yield: 20 slices

1 serving contains:

Cal	Prot	Fat	Chol	Carb	Fib	Sodium
73kc	2gm	1gm	trace	13gm	trace	142mg

Dinner Rolls

Always a holiday treat when I was growing up.

2 (1/4-oz.) pkgs. active dry yeast, about 2 tablespoons

1/2 cup warm water (110F, 45C)

1-3/4 cups skim milk, lukewarm

1/4 cup low-fat margarine, melted

1/4 cup sugar

1/2 tablespoon salt

6 cups or more unbleached or all-purpose flour

In a large mixing bowl, dissolve yeast in water. Add milk, margarine, sugar, salt and 4 cups flour. If you have a dough hook, use it. If not, mix and knead by hand. Add 2 cups flour, 1/2 cup at a time, until dough clings to hook and cleans side of bowl. Knead 8 to 10 minutes, adding flour when necessary to clean sides of bowl. When dough is smooth and elastic, place in a large lightly oiled bowl; cover with a cloth. Let rise in a warm place until doubled, about 1 hour. Press your finger into dough; if indentation remains, dough is ready. Punch down and let rise again until almost double, about 30 minutes. Spray a baking sheet with vegetable spray. Shape into rolls and place on prepared baking sheet. Cover and let rise until doubled, about 25 minutes. Preheat oven to 400F (205C). Bake 12 to 15 minutes or until golden brown.

Yield: 48 rolls

1 serving contains:

Cal	Prot	Fat	Chol	Carb	Fib	Sodium
69kc	2gm	1gm	trace	13gm	trace	78mg

How to Shape Rolls:

Parkerhouse Rolls: Place dough on a floured board and roll out until about 1/4-inch thick. Cut out with a biscuit cutter. Fold across so top half slightly overlaps bottom. Press edges together at fold. Place on an ungreased baking sheet.

Dinner Rolls: Pinch off dough and roll into balls about 1/3 the size desired. Place on an ungreased baking sheet; do not let rolls touch.

Soft Dinner Rolls: Pinch off dough and roll into balls about 1/3 the size desired. Place close together in a lightly oiled round pan.

Cloverleaf Rolls: Pinch off dough and roll into balls about 1-inch in diameter. Place 3 balls in each lightly greased muffin cup.

Crescent Rolls: Pinch off dough and roll into a cylindrical shape, tapering at each end. Place on an ungreased baking sheet and lightly shape dough into a crescent shape.

After shaping, all rolls need to raise until double in size. Bake at 400F (205C) 12 to 15 minutes or until lightly browned.

Cinnamon Rolls

Yummy Cinnamon rolls without the usual fat. Glaze with your favorite icing.

3/4 cup sugar

3 teaspoons ground cinnamon

1/2 recipe for Dinner Rolls, page 80

2 tablespoons low-fat margarine, room temperature

1-1/2 cups raisins

Combine sugar and cinnamon; set aside. After dough for Dinner Rolls has raised the second time, divide into 2 sections. Roll 1 section into an oblong about 12" x 9". Spread with 1 tablespoon margarine and half of sugar and cinnamon. Scatter with half of raisins over all. Roll up dough tightly, beginning at wide side. Seal edges by pinching together. Cut roll into 1-inch slices. Spray a round 8-inch pan with vegetable spray. Place dough slices in pan. Repeat for second half of dough. Cover and let rise about 45 minutes until doubled in bulk. Preheat oven to 350F (175C). Bake rolls 15 minutes or until lightly brown. Invert pan onto a plate; let stand 5 minutes before removing pan. Serve warm.

Yield: 16 rolls

1 roll without icing contains:

Cal	Prot	Fat	Chol	Carb	Fib	Sodium
184kc	4gm	2gm	trace	40gm	2gm	135mg

Pancakes

Vary these pancakes by adding 1/2 cup raisins or blueberries.

3 egg whites, slightly beaten

2 cups Baking Mix, page 65

About 1-1/4 cups skim milk

1/8 teaspoon oil of choice

In a medium-size bowl, combine egg whites, Baking Mix and 1 cup milk. Using a wire whisk or fork, mix just until blended; do not beat. Add remaining milk if needed to keep batter thin enough to pour. Pour oil into a non-stick griddle or skillet. Using a paper towel, spread oil around. Heat skillet over medium-high heat. Pour about 1/4 cup batter onto griddle (more or less batter acccording to your personal preference for thickness). Cook until pancake is covered with bubbles; turn and cook until lightly browned. Serve immediately.

Yield: 10 (5-1/2-inch) cakes

1 pancake contains:

Cal	Prot	Fat	Chol	Carb	Fib	Sodium
75kc	4gm	trace	1mg	14gm	trace	180mg

Basic Crepe Batter

Enjoy these no-cholesterol crepes filled with chicken.

2 egg whites

1/2 cup egg substitute (or the equivalent of 2 eggs)

1 cup unbleached or all-purpose flour

1/8 teaspoon salt

2 tablespoons non-fat powdered milk

1 cup water

Variation:

Dessert Crepe: To the above recipe add 2 tablespoons sugar, 1 tablespoon non-fat powdered milk and 1 teaspoon vanilla extract.

Combine egg whites and egg substitute. In a bowl, combine flour, salt and powdered milk. Add dry mixture alternately with water to eggs; beat until smooth. Cover and refrigerate at least 1 hour. Heat a non-stick crepe pan over medium heat. Brush a drop of oil around pan. Using a scoop or cup equivalent to 3 tablespoons, pour batter into pan. Immediately tilt pan, swirling batter to cover pan bottom evenly. Cook until bottom is brown and top appears dry. It is not necessary to cook the other side. Stack cooked crepes on a plate. When crepes are cooked, fill or store for later use. If you plan to refrigerate or freeze crepes, place waxed paper or foil between each one and wrap. Store in an air-tight container.

Yield: 15 crepes

1 crepe contains:

Cal	Prot	Fat	Chol	Carb	Fib	Sodium
42kc	3gm	trace	trace	7gm	trace	40mg

French Toast with Steamed Apples

A perfect brunch dish. Prepare ahead and arrange in a chafing dish to keep warm.

2 egg whites

1/2 cup egg substitute (equivalent of 2 eggs)

2/3 cup skim milk

1 tablespoon non-fat powdered milk

8 slices French bread, 3/4-inch thick

2 red cooking apples, cored, sliced

1/2 tablespoon water

1/2 teaspoon Butter Buds®

1/2 cup raisins

1 teaspoon oil of choice

3 tablespoons powdered sugar

In a medium-size bowl, combine egg whites, egg substitute, milk and powdered milk. Pour into a 13" x 9" pan. Place bread slices in egg mixture for 10 minutes; turn carefully. Let stand until liquid is absorbed. In a non-stick skillet over low heat, add apple slices and water. Cover and cook 10 minutes or until tender. Add Butter Buds® and raisins; cover and set aside. While apples are cooking, heat a large non-stick skillet over medium heat. Brush with 1/2 teaspoon oil. Gently lift 4 bread slices into skillet. Cook until lightly browned; turn and cook remaining side 4 to 5 minutes or until lightly browned. Repeat with remaining oil and bread. Arrange toast on a serving plate. Top with apples and raisins; sift powdered sugar over all. Serve immediately.

Yield: 4 servings (2 slices each)

1 serving contains:

Cal	Prot	Fat	Chol	Carb	Fib	Sodium
371kc	15gm	5gm	1mg	68gm	4gm	499mg

Salads

Salads can be the most versatile part of your menu. A dish like Chicken-Pasta Salad can be served as a lunch or supper main course, with Tomato-Onion Salad contributing a texture and color contrast as the side dish. Follow this with refreshing Fresh-Fruit Salad, and you will have given your guests a well-rounded and attractive meal. Provide the little bit of extra 'body' such a menu may require by offering delicious home-baked breads or rolls from your own oven, page 80, or a local bakery.

The only caution when planning a meal composed mainly of salads is to make sure foods are combined with a variety of dressings. If all your salads have a vinaigrette or mayonnaise-type dressing, there will be a sameness to the dishes no matter what the actual composition of the salad. A salad buffet is such a natural for summer entertaining, so it is worth looking for unusual dressing and sauce recipes throughout the year.

This section includes a wide variety of salads chosen for their nutritional value as well as taste and eye appeal.

Always make your salad with the freshest ingredients possible. The success of a tossed salad depends on the crispness of the greens and the freshness of other vegetables. The same holds true for fruit salads. How often have you been disappointed in the flavor of a basket of color-perfect strawberries once you get them home from the supermarket? Appearance is not always a guarantee with fruit. You may have to pay extra at a specialty produce market to get the best flavor and texture.

Carefully wash vegetables or fruit thoroughly with cold water. Drain in a colander, then on paper towels. When fairly dry, put in a plastic bag or plastic container and refrigerate. I don't wash my ingredients until the day I plan to use them.

Tossed salads can be made several hours ahead. Tear the lettuce instead of cutting it. Place all ingredients, except tomato, in a large bowl, and cover with a slightly damp cotton cloth until ready to serve.

Fresh fruit can be prepared ahead but must be treated with an ascorbic-acid mixture, such as Fruit Fresh®, or by dipping the cut fruit into lemon juice to prevent it turning brown.

Many salads are quick and easy to put together if you keep a variety of greens and other vegetables in the refrigerator. For an attractive, simple spinach salad, tear washed and dried spinach leaves and place on a salad plate. Garnish with tomato wedges and overlap a few red-onion rings on top of the spinach. Sprinkle a few toasted croutons over all and serve with John's Favorite Dressing.

The increased availability of low-fat cheeses and dressings makes it possible to enjoy your salad favorites like chef's salad. Plain low-fat yogurt can usually be substituted successfully for part of the mayonnaise or sour cream in a creamy dressing.

Try livening up a cottage-cheese-stuffed tomato with a sprinkling of chopped fresh herbs. These are available in many markets today and may go a long way toward making diet restrictions palatable. Another easy cottage-cheese idea is to use pears or peaches, canned in "lite" syrup, as the base. Spoon cottage cheese into the hollow of the fruit and top with chopped fresh mint.

To help you serve your family at least one salad course a day, here is a list of unusual and tasty salad ingredients. Use any of them together or combine with old favorites.

Artichoke hearts, not packed in oil
Asparagus, cooked
Bell peppers, roasted or raw
Broccoli
Cauliflower
Mushrooms, sliced or whole
Peas, fresh or frozen
Sprouts
Sugar snap peas
Summer squash
Water chestnuts
Zucchini

To roast bell or chili peppers, preheat oven to broil. Place peppers on a baking pan. Broil until skin blisters and starts to turn black, turning a few times to cook evenly. Place peppers in a paper bag, close bag and let stand a few minutes. Remove peppers from bag and peel off skin. These make a delicious addition to any salad or serve them alone with a simple vinaigrette dressing. You may want to protect your hands with rubber gloves when working with chiles.

Fresh-Fruit Salad

Use any combination of fruit. Add honey dressing when the fruit is not very flavorful; otherwise enjoy the fresh natural taste alone.

1/2 cantaloupe, cut into bite-size pieces

2 peaches, sliced

1 banana, cubed

2 tablespoons honey

1/2 teaspoon lemon juice

In a medium-size bowl, combine fruit. In a small bowl, blend honey and lemon juice; drizzle over fruit and toss gently to coat.

Yield: About 10 (1/2-cup) servings

1 serving contains:

Cal	Prot	Fat	Chol	Carb	Fib	Sodium
43kc	1gm	trace	0	11gm	1gm	3mg

Variation:

Cottage Cheese & Fresh-Fruit Salad:
Spoon fruit into individual lettuce-lined serving dishes. Top fruit with 1/3 cup low-fat cottage cheese and garnish with sliced fresh strawberries.

Mixed Fruit with Coconut Pudding

Exotic taste of coconut without the fat.

1 cup skim milk

1 (3.5-oz.) pkg. instant vanilla pudding

1/8 teaspoon imitation coconut flavoring

1/2 cup plain low-fat yogurt

1 (8-oz.) can crushed pineapple, not drained

1 (11-oz.) can mandarin oranges, drained

1 (16-oz.) can peaches, sliced, drained

In a large bowl, combine milk, pudding mix, coconut flavoring and yogurt. Add fruit and toss gently. Cover and refrigerate a few hours until ready to serve.

Yield: 10 (1/2-cup) servings

1 serving contains:

Cal	Prot	Fat	Chol	Carb	Fib	Sodium
85kc	2gm	trace	1mg	19gm	trace	168mg

Variation:

Mixed Fruit with Lemon Pudding: Substitute instant lemon pudding for vanilla pudding and omit coconut flavoring.

Special-Occasion Three-Bean Salad

A great dish for potlucks.

1-1/2 cups cooked white beans, drained

1-1/2 cups cooked kidney beans, drained

1-1/2 cups cooked green beans, drained

1/3 cup finely diced celery

1/3 cup sliced green onion

1/3 cup oil of choice

2 tablespoons wine vinegar

1 teaspoon Italian seasoning

1/2 teaspoon dried leaf tarragon

3 pkgs. artificial sweetener, optional

In a large bowl, combine all ingredients, tossing gently to coat all vegetables. Cover and refrigerate several hours or overnight. To serve, spoon salad into an attractive serving bowl.

Yield: 12 (1/2-cup) servings

1 serving contains:

Cal	Prot	Fat	Chol	Carb	Fib	Sodium
116kc	4gm	6gm	0	12gm	3gm	152mg

California Chicken Salad

Garnish individual salad plates with a fan of papaya slices and some spinach leaves for a cool, refreshing look.

5 cups diced cooked chicken

2 cups pineapple tidbits, packed in natural juice, drained

1 cup diced celery

1/2 cup chopped onion

1/2 cup plain low-fat yogurt

1 cup low-fat mayonnaise-type salad dressing

1/2 teaspoon curry powder

Red-leaf lettuce to garnish

In a large bowl, combine chicken, pineapple, celery and onion. In a small bowl, combine yogurt, salad dressing and curry powder; blend well. Pour over chicken mixture, tossing to coat all pieces well. Refrigerate 2 to 3 hours until ready to serve. To serve, arrange salad on a platter lined with red-leaf lettuce.

Yield: 10 (1-cup) servings

1 serving contains:

Cal	Prot	Fat	Chol	Carb	Fib	Sodiuim
145kc	17gm	5gm	48mg	9gm	trace	128mg

Coleslaw

Like my mom used to make! Bell-pepper
rings make an attractive garnish.

3 cups shredded cabbage

1 small carrot, shredded

1/2 teaspoon vinegar

1 tablespoon sugar

2 tablespoons skim milk

1/3 cup low-fat mayonnaise-type
salad dressing

Dash of pepper

In a medium-size bowl, combine
cabbage and carrot. In a small bowl,
mix vinegar, sugar, milk, salad dressing
and pepper. Pour over cabbage and toss
gently until well-coated. Refrigerate 2 to
3 hours until ready to serve. To serve,
transfer coleslaw to a serving bowl.

Yield: 6 (1/2-cup) servings

1 serving contains:

Cal	Prot	Fat	Chol	Carb	Fib	Sodium
43kc	1gm	2gm	2mg	8gm	1gm	54mg

Marinated Cucumbers

Make this sweet-tart salad the day before you serve it. For additional color and texture, add pimiento strips and alfalfa sprouts just before serving.

1/2 cup vinegar

2 tablespoons water

2 pkgs. artificial sweetener

Salt and pepper to taste

2 medium-size cucumbers, thinly sliced

1/2 teaspoon dill weed

In a small saucepan, bring vinegar, water, sweetener, salt and pepper to a boil. Reduce heat and simmer about 10 minutes; cool. Pour marinade over cucumbers in a serving bowl. Sprinkle with dill. Refrigerate several hours before serving.

Yield: 4 (1/2-cup) servings

1 serving contains:

Cal	Prot	Fat	Chol	Carb	Fib	Sodium
13kc	trace	trace	0	4gm	1gm	4mg

Tuna-Rice Salad

Ideal for a light, cool summer luncheon. Add sugar peas and cherry tomatoes for an attractive edible garnish.

1 (6-1/2-oz.) can white tuna, packed in water

2 cups cooked long-grain rice

1 cup peas, cooked

1/2 cup diced low-fat Swiss cheese

1 tablespoon chopped fresh parsley

1/2 cup low-fat mayonnaise-type salad dressing

1/2 teaspoon dry mustard

1/2 teaspoon wine vinegar

1/4 teaspoon pepper

Leaf lettuce

Drain tuna well; place in a medium-size bowl. Break apart tuna with a fork. Add rice, peas, cheese and parsley. In a small bowl, blend salad dressing, mustard, vinegar and pepper. Pour over tuna mixture, tossing gently to mix well. To serve, arrange on a lettuce-lined platter.

Yield: 4 (1-cup) servings

1 serving contains:

Cal	Prot	Fat	Chol	Carb	Fib	Sodium
272kc	21gm	7gm	28mg	35gm	3gm	311mg

Tuna Salad

Use for tuna-salad sandwiches—an old favorite for lunch.

1 (6-1/2-oz.) can white tuna, packed in water

2 tablespoons low-fat mayonnaise-type salad dressing

1 tablespoon finely chopped celery

1 tablespoon pickle relish

1 hardcooked egg

Drain tuna well; place in a small bowl. Break apart tuna with a fork. Peel egg and discard yolk; dice white. Add salad dressing, celery, relish and egg white; toss gently to combine. Use as desired.

Yield: 2 (1/2-cup) servings

Serving Suggestions:

Use to stuff fresh tomatoes, then serve on a bed of spinach with alfalfa sprouts.

Boil eggs; discard yolk. Stuff egg centers with tuna salad and arrange on a bed of greens. Garnish with cherry tomatoes.

1 serving contains:

Cal	Prot	Fat	Chol	Carb	Fib	Sodium
157kc	28gm	4gm	34mg	5gm	trace	469mg

Tropical Tuna Salad

A fun and easy nutritious lunch.

1 (20-oz.) can pineapple chunks, packed in natural juice, drained

2 (6-1/2-oz.) cans white tuna, packed in water, flaked

1/2 cup coarsely chopped green bell pepper

2 tablespoons chopped pimientos

1/2 cup low-fat mayonnaise-type salad dressing

2 bananas, sliced

1 medium-size head lettuce, washed, drained

In a large bowl, combine pineapple, tuna, bell pepper, pimiento and salad dressing. Toss gently to mix, then refrigerate 2 to 3 hours until ready to serve. To serve, add sliced bananas and toss gently to mix. Cut head of lettuce into 6 wedges. Lay each wedge on a luncheon plate and spoon tuna salad alongside lettuce.

Yield: 6 (1-cup) servings

1 serving contains:

Cal	Prot	Fat	Chol	Carb	Fib	Sodium
187kc	19gm	4gm	24mg	22gm	2gm	291mg

Asparagus Salad

An elegant salad for a special dinner.

**24 asparagus stalks, washed, tough
ends removed**

1/4 cup no-oil Italian salad dressing

**2 tablespoons grated Parmesan
cheese**

In a large kettle with a steamer, steam
asparagus 4 to 5 minutes or until crisp-
tender. Remove asparagus from
steamer; drain well. Gently place
asparagus in a large shallow dish. Pour
salad dressing over asparagus; cover
and refrigerate 2 to 3 hours until ready
to serve. To serve, arrange asparagus on
individual plates, laying 5 spears in one
direction and setting sixth spear at a
right angle on top. Spoon salad dressing
over asparagus; sprinkle with cheese.

Yield: 4 servings

1 serving contains:

Cal	Prot	Fat	Chol	Carb	Fib	Sodium
72kc	6gm	2gm	3mg	8gm	2gm	184mg

Cabbage Salad

Perfect salad for a crowd.

2 teaspoons all-purpose flour

1-1/2 cups sugar

1 cup vinegar

1 tablespoon low-fat margarine

1/2 teaspoon ground tumeric

1 teaspoon salt

**1 medium head of cabbage,
  shredded, about 7 cups**

**3/4 cup finely chopped green bell
  pepper**

3/4 cup finely chopped onion

1 cup finely chopped celery

In a large saucepan, combine flour and sugar; add vinegar and margarine. Stir over medium heat until sugar is dissolved. Add tumeric, salt, cabbage, green pepper, onion and celery. Heat through, stirring constantly; do not boil. Cool, then cover and refrigerate at least overnight before serving. This salad will keep well for several days.

Yield: 11 (1-cup) servings

1 serving contains:

Cal	Prot	Fat	Chol	Carb	Fib	Sodium
129kc	1gm	1gm	0	33gm	2gm	212mg

Frozen-Cabbage Salad

Keep several containers in the freezer.

1 medium head of cabbage, finely shredded, about 7 cups

1/2 tablespoon salt

3/4 cup chopped green bell pepper

3/4 cup chopped celery

3 cups sugar

1-1/2 cups vinegar

3/4 cup water

1/4 teaspoon ground cloves

1-1/2 teaspoon mustard seed

1-1/2 teaspoon celery seed

In a large bowl, place shredded cabbage and sprinkle with salt; let stand 1 hour. Drain well. Add green pepper and celery; toss gently. In a medium-size saucepan, combine sugar, vinegar, water, cloves, mustard seed and celery seed. Bring to a boil and boil 1 minute. Immediately pour over cabbage mixture. Pack in sterile freezer containers, making sure syrup covers top of cabbage; freeze up to 6 months. Thaw in the refrigerator as needed. This salad will keep several days in the refrigerator.

Yield: 18 (1/2-cup) servings

1 serving contains:

Cal	Prot	Fat	Chol	Carb	Fib	Sodium
135kc	1gm	trace	0	36gm	1gm	175mg

Carolyn's Cauliflower Salad

Always a favorite at luncheons.

4 cups cauliflowerets

1/2 cup diced onion

1 cup low-fat mayonnaise-type salad dressing

1/2 cup shredded low-fat cheddar cheese

1/3 cup imitation bacon bits (no fat)

In a clear glass bowl, layer cauliflowerets and onions. Carefully spread salad dressing over vegetables. Sprinkle cheese, then bacon bits over vegetables. Cover and refrigerate overnight for flavors to blend. Before serving, toss to mix.

Yield: 10 (1/2-cup) servings

1 serving contains:

Cal	Prot	Fat	Chol	Carb	Fib	Sodium
83kc	4gm	1gm	7mg	8gm	1gm	200mg

Cranberry-Orange Salad

Delicious for holidays or any day.

1 (11-oz.) can mandarin oranges with juice

1 pkg. unflavored gelatin

2 tablespoons sugar

1 (16-oz.) can whole-cranberry sauce

1/2 cup finely chopped celery

Variation:

If your diet allows, add 1/4 cup finely chopped nuts with oranges.

Drain oranges well; set aside juice and oranges. In a small saucepan, mix gelatin and sugar; stir in juice from oranges. Stir over low heat until dissolved. Transfer to a bowl and refrigerate. When gelatin mixture begins to set, stir in cranberries, oranges and celery. Spoon into a serving container. Refrigerate several hours or until firm.

Yield: 6 (1/2-cup) servings

Serving suggestions:

Salad can be made in a decorative mold, individual molds or a loaf pan, then unmolded onto a bed of lettuce.

1 serving contains:

Cal	Prot	Fat	Chol	Carb	Fib	Sodium
148kc	1gm	trace	0	35gm	1gm	34mg

Sparkling Fruit Cup

A colorful, sparkling summer salad.

1 cup honeydew-melon balls or bite-size pieces

1 cup watermelon balls or bite-size pieces

1 cup Bing cherries, pitted

1 cup grapes

1 tablespoon snipped fresh mint

1 cup lemon-lime carbonated beverage

In a medium bowl, combine fruit and mint; refrigerate 2 to 3 hours until ready to serve. Immediately before serving, spoon fruit mixture into individual serving dishes. Slowly pour lemon-lime beverage over fruit.

Yield: 8 (1/2-cup) servings

1 serving contains:

Cal	Prot	Fat	Chol	Carb	Fib	Sodium
40kc	trace	trace	0	10gm	1gm	5mg

Macaroni Salad

Perfect dish for a patio party.

2 cups elbow macaroni

4 hard-cooked eggs

1/3 cup sliced green onion

1/3 cup diced celery

1/3 cup chopped dill pickles

1 (4-oz.) jar pimiento

1/2 teaspoon salt

1/4 teaspoon pepper

Dash of paprika

Dressing:

3 tablespoons sugar

1 teaspoon cider vinegar

2 teaspoons yellow mustard

1 cup low-fat mayonnaise-type salad dressing

Cook macaroni according to package directions; drain. Peel eggs and discard yolks; dice whites. In a large bowl, combine macaroni, egg whites, green onion, celery, pickles, pimiento, salt and pepper; set aside. To make dressing, combine sugar, vinegar, mustard and salad dressing in a small bowl; stir well to blend. Pour dressing over salad. Cover and refrigerate until chilled. When ready to serve, lightly dust with paprika.

Yield: 14 (1/2-cup) servings

1 serving contains:

Cal	Prot	Fat	Chol	Carb	Fib	Sodium
74kc	2gm	2gm	2mg	13gm	trace	213mg

Orangy Beets

A colorful addition to any meal.

6 pkgs. artificial sweetener

1/2 cup cider vinegar

1 bay leaf

1/2 cup orange juice

**1 (16-oz.) can beets, drained,
quartered or sliced**

In a small saucepan, combine sweetener, vinegar and bay leaf. Bring to a boil; reduce heat and simmer 5 minutes. Remove from heat; stir in orange juice, then pour over beets in a medium bowl. Cover and refrigerate several hours before serving.

Yield: 4 (1/2-cup) servings

1 serving contains:

Cal	Prot	Fat	Chol	Carb	Fib	Sodium
56kc	1gm	trace	0	15gm	3gm	326mg

Sylvia's Orange-Gelatin Salad

Carrots and pineapple make it high in vitamin A.

1 (.6-oz.) pkg. sugar-free orange gelatin

2 cups boiling water

1 cup cold water

1 (8-oz.) can crushed pineapple, packed in natural juice, not drained

1/2 cup white raisins

3/4 cup shredded carrot

In a large bowl, combine gelatin with boiling water, stirring until gelatin is dissolved. Stir in cold water, pineapple and pineapple juice. Refrigerate until gelatin starts to set. Add raisins and carrot. Pour into a shallow 9-inch-square dish. Refrigerate several hours or overnight until gelatin is firm.

Yield: 9 (1/2-cup) servings

1 serving contains:

Cal	Prot	Fat	Chol	Carb	Fib	Sodium
43kc	1gm	trace	0	9gm	1gm	58mg

Pasta Primavera

Variety of vegetables makes a colorful, nutritious salad.

2 cups macaroni, elbow or shells

1/2 tablespoon olive oil

1 garlic clove, minced

2 cups raw vegetables, cut for stir-frying

About 1 cup no-oil Italian salad dressing

Cherry tomatoes for garnish

Suggested vegetables for stir-frying:

Broccoli
Carrots
Cauliflower
Green bell pepper
Onion
Zucchini

Cook macaroni according to package directions; drain. In a wok or large non-stick skillet, heat oil until it sizzles. Stir garlic in oil 3 or 4 seconds, then add vegetables. Stir-fry 1 to 2 minutes on high heat, then reduce heat to medium-high. Cook 1 to 2 minutes longer or until crisp-tender. Place macaroni in a large serving bowl; add stir-fried vegetables. Pour salad dressing over all, tossing gently to coat all pieces well. Refrigerate 2 to 6 hours until ready to serve. It may be necessary to add more dressing before serving. To serve, garnish with cherry tomatoes.

Yield: Approximately 8 (1-cup) servings

1 serving contains:

Cal	Prot	Fat	Chol	Carb	Fib	Sodium
145kc	4gm	4gm	2mg	23gm	1gm	243mg

Pickled Beets & Onions

A crunchy, colorful side dish.

1 cup vinegar

1/2 cup water

1 cup beet juice from can

2 tablespoons sugar or 4 pkgs. artificial sweetener

2 tablespoons pickling spice

1 (16-oz.) can beets, drained, quartered

2 cups thinly sliced onions

In a medium saucepan, combine vinegar, water, beet juice, sugar or sweetener and pickling spice. Bring to a boil; reduce heat and simmer about 10 minutes. Strain and cool. Pour over beets and onions in a medium bowl. Refrigerate several hours before serving.

Yield: 8 (1/2-cup) servings

1 serving contains:

Cal	Prot	Fat	Chol	Carb	Fib	Sodium
39kc	1gm	trace	0	11gm	2gm	22mg

Grandma's Potato Salad

Deliciously creamy.

8 medium potatoes, boiled with skin on

3 hard-cooked eggs

1/3 cup diced celery

1/3 cup diced onion

1/3 cup chopped sweet pickles

1 (4-oz.) jar pimiento, chopped

1/2 teaspoon salt

1/4 teaspoon pepper

Dash of paprika

Dressing:

3 tablespoons sugar

1 teaspoon cider vinegar

2 teaspoon yellow mustard

1 cup low-fat mayonnaise-type salad dressing

Peel and dice potatoes while warm; put in a large bowl. Peel eggs and discard yolks; dice whites and add to potatoes. Add celery, onion, pickles, pimiento, salt and pepper; toss gently. In a small bowl, combine sugar, vinegar, mustard and salad dressing; blend well. Pour over vegetables; toss gently to coat. Dressing coats best if potatoes are still warm. Sprinkle with paprika. Refrigerate at least 1 hour before serving.

Yield: Approximately 8 (1-cup) servings

1 serving contains:

Cal	Prot	Fat	Chol	Carb	Fib	Sodium
238kc	4gm	8gm	10mg	38gm	2gm	216mg

Curried Chicken & Pasta Salad

Looks most attractive garnished with melon or pineapple wedges.

2 boneless, skinless whole-chicken breasts, about 1 lb.

1/4 cup white wine

1/2 teaspoon dried-leaf thyme

1 carrot, quartered

1/2 onion, quartered

3/4 cup water

1/4 teaspoon salt

1/2 cup uncooked pasta

2 cups seedless grapes

1/4 cup thinly sliced celery

1/4 cup thinly sliced green onion

2-1/2 tablespoons plain low-fat yogurt

3/4 cup low-fat mayonnaise-type salad dressing

1-1/2 tablespoons honey

1-1/2 teaspoons lemon juice

1/4 teaspoon curry powder

1/2 teaspoon salt

Lettuce to garnish

Place chicken in a medium saucepan with wine, thyme, carrot, onion, water and salt. Bring to boil, reduce heat and simmer, covered, about 45 minutes or until chicken is tender. Cool chicken in broth. Cook pasta according to package directions; drain. When chicken is cool, cut into 1-inch cubes and place in a large bowl with grapes, celery, green onion and pasta. In a small bowl, blend yogurt, salad dressing, honey, lemon juice, curry powder, salt and pepper. Pour over chicken mixture and toss. To serve, line a platter or serving bowl with lettuce leaves and spoon chicken salad onto lettuce.

Yield: 8 (3/4-cup) servings

1 serving contains:

Cal	Prot	Fat	Chol	Carb	Fib	Sodium
168kc	15gm	5gm	40mg	18gm	1gm	293mg

Sue's Chicken Salad

Crunchy and colorful: looks and tastes good.

1-1/2 cups grated carrots

1/2 cup raisins

1-1/2 cups cooked chicken breast, cubed

2 cups leaf lettuce, torn into bite-size pieces

1 cup iceburg lettuce, torn into bite-size pieces

1/2 cup plain low-fat yogurt

1 tablespoon honey

Variation:

If your diet allows, add 3/4 cup chopped walnuts.

In a large salad bowl, combine carrots, raisins, chicken and lettuce. In a small bowl, blend yogurt and honey; drizzle over salad, tossing lightly. Serve immediately.

Yield: 8 (1-cup) servings

1 serving contains:

Cal	Prot	Fat	Chol	Carb	Fib	Sodium
92kc	8gm	1gm	19mg	13gm	2gm	36mg

Pennsylvania Dutch Tomatoes & Onions

A festive, colorful summer dish.

3 medium tomatoes, sliced

1 medium sweet onion, thinly sliced

1/2 cup lightly packed brown sugar

1/4 cup vinegar, white or flavored

3 parsley sprigs

In a medium-size shallow glass dish, alternate layers of tomatoes and onion until all vegetables are used. Sprinkle brown sugar over top, then slowly pour vinegar over sugar. Cover and refrigerate 3 to 4 hours until ready to serve. While salad is in refrigerator, spoon dressing over vegetables at least twice. Garnish with parsley sprigs before serving.

Yield: 8 (1/2-cup) servings

1 serving contains:

Cal	Prot	Fat	Chol	Carb	Fib	Sodium
69kc	1gm	trace	0	17gm	1gm	9mg

Clara's Sweet-Tart Vegetable Salad

This colorful dish can take the place of rice, potatoes or vegetables in your meal.

1 (16-oz.) can French-style green beans, drained

1 (12-oz.) can white corn, drained

1 (17-oz.) can tiny peas, drained

1 cup chopped celery

1/4 cup chopped green onion

1 cup chopped green bell pepper

1 (2-oz.) jar pimiento, chopped

Dressing:

3/4 cup vinegar

About 1/2 cup oil of choice

1/2 cup sugar

4 pkgs. artificial sweetener

1 teaspoon celery seed

Pepper to taste

In a large bowl, combine vegetables. To make dressing, in a small saucepan, stir ingredients over medium-low heat just until sugar is dissolved. Cool, then pour over vegetables. Cover and refrigerate at least overnight or several days.

Yield: 16 (1/2-cup) servings

1 serving contains:

Cal	Prot	Fat	Chol	Carb	Fib	Sodium
135kc	2gm	7gm	0	17gm	2gm	138mg

Waldorf Salad

Begin with fresh greens and apples for a successful salad.

3 cups lettuce, torn into bite-size pieces

1 Rome apple, cored, cut into bite-size pieces

1/2 cup raisins

1/2 cup plain low-fat yogurt

1/2 cup low-fat mayonnaise-type salad dressing

Dash of ground cinnamon

Dash of ground nutmeg

In a large bowl, combine lettuce, apple and raisins. In a small bowl, blend yogurt, salad dressing, cinnamon and nutmeg. Pour over salad and toss gently until lettuce is coated. Serve immediately.

Yield: 9 (1/2-cup) servings

1 serving contains:

Cal	Prot	Fat	Chol	Carb	Fib	Sodium
61kc	1gm	2gm	3mg	12gm	1gm	51mg

Wilted Lettuce

A family favorite.

1 head leaf lettuce, rinsed, dried

1/3 cup chopped green onion

1/4 cup white vinegar

1/2 cup water

2 tablespoons oil of choice

1 teaspoon sugar

In a large bowl, separate lettuce leaves and tear into bite-size pieces; add green onion. In a small saucepan, combine vinegar, water, oil and sugar; bring to a boil. Pour over lettuce and onion; toss gently to coat lettuce well. Serve immediately.

Yield: 6 (1-cup) servings

1 serving contains:

Cal	Prot	Fat	Chol	Carb	Fib	Sodium
48kc	trace	5gm	0	2gm	trace	2mg

Creamy Dressing

Great with leaf lettuce, tomato and croutons.

1 cup low-fat mayonnaise-type salad dressing

1/4 cup catsup

Dash of red-pepper sauce

1/8 teaspoon vinegar

In a small bowl, blend all ingredients. Let stand briefly before serving to blend flavors.

Yield: 10 (2-tablespoon) servings

1 serving contains:

Cal	Prot	Fat	Chol	Carb	Fib	Sodium
38kc	0	3gm	3mg	5gm	0	133mg

John's Favorite Dressing

Sweet-and-sour dressing—great with spinach salad.

1 teaspoon unflavored gelatin

1 cup water

1/4 cup vinegar

2 tablespoons finely chopped onion

1/4 cup sugar plus 3 pkgs. artificial sweetener

1/3 cup catsup

2 teaspoons Worcestershire sauce

In a small bowl, mix gelatin with about 2 tablespoons water; set aside. In a blender, combine vinegar, onion, sugar, sweetener, catsup and Worcestershire sauce. Mix remaining water with softened gelatin and add to other ingredients in blender; blend well. Refrigerate about 1 hour or until slightly thickened. Shake well before serving.

Yield: 16 (2-tablespoon) servings

1 serving contains:

Cal	Prot	Fat	Chol	Carb	Fib	Sodium
19kc	trace	trace	0	5gm	trace	59mg

Sweet-&-Sour Dressing

Perfect for a variety of salads.

3 tablespoons sugar

1 teaspoon vinegar

2 teaspoons prepared yellow mustard

1 cup low-fat mayonnaise-type salad dressing

In a small bowl, combine all ingredients. Refrigerate before using.

Yield: 10 (2-tablespoon) servings

1 serving contains:

Cal	Prot	Fat	Chol	Carb	Fib	Sodium
47kc	0	3gm	3mg	7gm	0	83mg

Tart Horseradish Dressing

Lower in fat and calories than commercial dressing.

1/2 cup plain low-fat yogurt

1/2 cup low-fat mayonnaise-type salad dressing

2 tablespoons minced dill pickle

1/2 teaspoon prepared horseradish

1/4 teaspoon prepared brown mustard

1/4 cup catsup

Dash of teriyaki sauce

In a small bowl, combine all ingredients; mix well. Cover and refrigerate several hours before serving.

Yield: 10 (2-tablespoon) servings

1 serving contains:

Cal	Prot	Fat	Chol	Carb	Fib	Sodium
30kc	1gm	2gm	2mg	4gm	0	203mg

Vinegar & Oil Dressing

Classic dressing made low-calorie and low-fat.

3/4 cup water

1/4 cup vinegar

2 tablespoons honey

1 tablespoon oil of choice

Combine ingredients in a cruet; shake well.

Yield: 10 (2-tablespoon) servings

1 serving contains:

Cal	Prot	Fat	Chol	Carb	Fib	Sodium
26kc	0	1gm	0	4gm	0	trace

Poultry

Poultry is one of our favorite foods. It's nutritious because it's high in protein, B vitamins and minerals. With the exception of duck and goose, it is fairly low in fat and can be made more so by removing skin and any visible fat before cooking.

Chicken is probably the most versatile food in your kitchen. It can be prepared in a wide variety of ways, such as roasting, stove-top casseroles, oven casseroles or broiling. I believe a clay pot does a wonderful job of "roasting" a chicken, and roast chicken is a remarkably easy dish to prepare.

With all my recipes, you can sauté or stir-fry chicken in a non-stick skillet with a minimum amount of oil. It is not necessary to have the large quantity of oil traditionally used for these dishes.

Turkey is available at the market in many forms year-round. With a little experimentation, you can substitute ground turkey or chicken for ground beef in many of your favorite recipes—it is a welcome change. Turkey breasts have also become quite popular. They are quick and simple to prepare and can provide a great dinner as well as delicious sandwiches for another day.

In this section, you will find a large selection of recipes for varied styles and tastes.

Broiled Turkey Cutlets

A quick, flavorful change. Strips of Roasted Red Bell Peppers, page 89, make an eye-catching garnish.

4 turkey-breast cutlets, about 8 oz.

1 tablespoon olive oil

2 tablespoons lime juice

1 tablespoon soy sauce

1 small garlic clove, minced

2 tablespoons minced onion

1 tablespoon minced cilantro or parsley

Pepper to taste

Rinse turkey and pat dry. In a small bowl, combine oil, lime juice, soy sauce, garlic, onion, cilantro or parsley and pepper. Pour over turkey cutlets in a large shallow dish; cover and marinate in refrigerator 2 hours. Preheat oven to broil. Remove cutlets from marinade to a broiler pan, reserving marinade. Broil cutlets 4 to 5 inches from source of heat about 2 minutes on each side or until just tender, basting twice with reserved marinade; do not overcook. Serve immediately.

Yield: 2 servings

1 serving contains:

Cal	Prot	Fat	Chol	Carb	Fib	Sodium
205kc	28gm	9gm	68mg	4gm	trace	587mg

Chicken Breasts with Cling Peaches

If fresh peaches are available, use them. Substitute water for the canned peach juice.

2 chicken breasts, halved, skinned

1/2 cup all-purpose flour

1/2 teaspoon salt

Pepper to taste

4 canned cling-peach halves, packed in natural juice, drained, juice reserved

2 tablespoons brown sugar

2 tablespoons Marsala wine

1 teaspoon dried leaf basil

1/4 teaspoon ground allspice

Preheat oven to 350F (175C). Rinse chicken and pat dry. On a large plate, combine flour, salt and pepper. Dredge chicken in flour mixture; set aside. Heat a large non-stick skillet over medium-high heat; spray lightly with vegetable spray. Add chicken and cook quickly until browned on both sides. Place in a medium-size shallow baking dish. Arrange drained peach halves around chicken; set pan aside. Measure reserved peach liquid and make up to 1 cup using water; pour into a small bowl, stir in brown sugar, wine, basil and allspice. Pour over chicken and peaches; cover with a lid or foil. Bake about 45 minutes or until tender. To serve, place chicken and peaches on a serving plate and spoon over juices from dish.

Yield: 4 servings

1 serving contains:

Cal	Prot	Fat	Chol	Carb	Fib	Sodium
252kc	29gm	3gm	73mg	24gm	1gm	313mg

Chicken Breast with Apricots & Prunes

A wonderful fruity combination.

2 chicken breasts, halved, skinned

1/2 cup dried apricots

1/2 cup dried prunes

1/2 tablespoon apricot liqueur

1/2 tablespoon oil

1/2 cup apple juice

1 teaspoon lemon juice

1/4 cup white wine

1/4 cup chicken broth

2 tablespoons cold water

1 tablespoon cornstarch

Preheat oven to 350F(175C). Rinse chicken and pat dry. Heat a medium size non-stick skillet on medium-high heat. Spray 2-3 seconds with vegetable spray, add chicken and cook until browned on both sides. Put chicken into a 10-inch shallow baking dish, add apricots and prunes, set aside. In a small mixing bowl, combine liqueur, oil, juices and wine. Pour over chicken and fruit, cover and bake in a 350F oven for 45-50 minutes or until chicken is just tender. Pour pan drippings into a small saucepan; add chicken broth. In a small bowl combine water and cornstarch; stir into liquid in pan. Cook over medium-high heat, stirring constantly, until bubbly and thickened. Place chicken and fruit on serving platter; pour sauce over chicken.

Yield: 4 servings

1 serving contains:

Cal	Prot	Fat	Chol	Carb	Fib	Sodium
279kc	28gm	5gm	73mg	29gm	3gm	115mg

Fruit-Stuffed Turkey Tenderloins

Serve with broiled tomato halves and bright-green sugar-snap peas for a company dish.

2 fresh turkey-breast tenderloins, about 1-1/4 lbs.

Salt and pepper to taste

1/3 cup cubed fresh bread

1/2 cup finely diced cooking apple

1/3 cup finely diced prunes

1/4 teaspoon ground allspice

1/4 teaspoon ground nutmeg

2 tablespoons plus 1 teaspoon low-fat margarine, melted

Dash of paprika

Variations

Substitute 4 boneless, skinless chicken-breast halves for turkey tenderloins. Pound chicken until thin before wrapping each half around 1/4 of stuffing.

Preheat oven to 350F (175C). Rinse turkey and pat dry. Using kitchen shears, cut a pocket lengthwise in thickest side of each tenderloin. Salt and pepper inside of pockets; set aside. In a small bowl, combine bread, apple, prunes, allspice and nutmeg. Pour 2 tablespoons margarine over all, tossing well to coat bread cubes. Spoon stuffing into turkey pockets and secure with wooden picks. Place in a medium-size shallow baking dish. Drizzle 1 teaspoon melted margarine over turkey; dust lightly with paprika. Bake, covered, 45 to 50 minutes or just until turkey is tender, top and bottom. Baste occasionally with juices. To serve, cut each tenderloin in half.

Yield: 4 servings

1 serving contains:

Cal	Prot	Fat	Chol	Carb	Fib	Sodium
259kc	34gm	8gm	86mg	13gm	2gm	253mg

Creamy Chicken Casserole

Substitute turkey for chicken in this fla-
vorful casserole. Orangy Beets, page
106, make a lovely accompaniment.

2 tablespoons all-purpose flour

1 tablespoon non-fat powdered milk

1-1/4 cups skim milk

1/4 teaspoon salt

Pepper to taste

1/2 teaspoon dried-leaf marjoram

1/2 teaspoon dried-leaf thyme

**1/2 cup celery, thinly sliced
   diagonally**

1/2 cup fresh sliced mushrooms

**1 cup plus 1 tablespoon chicken
   broth**

3 cups cooked rice

2-1/2 cups cubed cooked chicken

1 tablespoon chopped fresh parsley

Variation

Diet permiting, sprinkle with 1/4 cup
   slivered almonds before baking.

Preheat oven to 350F (175C). In a
medium saucepan, combine flour and
powdered milk. Slowly add skim milk,
stirring to blend. Cook over medium
heat until sauce thickens, stirring constantly. Add salt, pepper, marjoram and
thyme; set aside. In a large non-stick
skillet over low heat, cook celery and
mushrooms in 1 tablespoon broth until
tender. Stir in rice, 1 cup broth, chicken
and sauce. Pour into a shallow casserole. Sprinkle with parsley. Bake, covered, 35 minutes; remove lid and bake
about 10 minutes longer or until bubbling. Serve immediately.

Yield: 6 servings

1 serving contains:

Cal	Prot	Fat	Chol	Carb	Fib	Sodium
224kc	19gm	2gm	38mg	31gm	1gm	293mg

Cathy's Baked Chicken

A different approach to baked chicken.

2 chicken breasts, halved, skinned

1 cup fresh bread crumbs

1/2 teaspoon onion powder

1/2 teaspoon garlic powder

1/4 teaspoon cayenne pepper

1/8 teaspoon ground ginger

1/3 cup plain low-fat yogurt

Variation

Substitute 1/4 cup oat bran for 1/4 cup
bread crumbs.

Preheat oven to 400F (205C). Lightly
spray a medium-size shallow baking
dish with vegetable spray. Rinse
chicken and pat dry. In a shallow pan,
combine bread crumbs, onion powder,
garlic powder, cayenne pepper and ginger. Dip chicken in yogurt, then into
crumb mixture. Place in prepared dish.
Bake, uncovered, 45 to 50 minutes or
until tender. Serve immediately.

Yield: 4 servings

1 serving contains:

Cal	Prot	Fat	Chol	Carb	Fib	Sodium
254kc	31gm	5gm	74mg	20gm	0	260mg

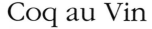

Coq au Vin

My "impress-the-guest" dish served with Rice & Pecan Pilaf, page 217, petite peas and Dinner Rolls, page 80. Although traditionally red wine is used in this classic dish, I prefer the flavor and color of white wine.

2 boneless chicken breasts, halved, skinned

4 teaspoons low-fat margarine

1/8 teaspoon garlic powder

1/8 teaspoon dried-leaf thyme

1/8 teaspoon lemon pepper

1/2 teaspoon minced chives

1 tablespoon chopped fresh parsley

1 tablespoon all-purpose flour

4 oz. fresh mushrooms, sliced

4 oz. pearl onions

1/4 cup white wine

Preheat oven to 350F (175C). Rinse chicken and pat dry. Melt 2 teaspoons margarine in a large non-stick skillet over medium heat. Add garlic powder and herbs; stir together 30 seconds. Dredge chicken in flour. Add to skillet and cook until brown on both sides. Remove to a small casserole; set aside. Add remaining 2 teaspoons margarine to skillet. Add mushrooms and onions; sauté until golden. Add to casserole. Pour wine into skillet and scrape up browned pieces. Pour over chicken. Bake, covered, 50 to 60 minutes or until tender. Serve immediately.

Yield: 4 servings

1 serving contains:

Cal	Prot	Fat	Chol	Carb	Fib	Sodium
193kc	28gm	5gm	73mg	5gm	1gm	112mg

Angie's Baked Chicken

Deliciously moist, quick and easy. Coleslaw, page 94, is a perfect accompaniment.

2 chicken breasts, halved, skinned

1 cup fine fresh bread crumbs

3/4 teaspoon paprika

3/4 teaspoon onion powder

1/4 teaspoon lemon pepper

1 tablespoon oil of choice

Variation

Substitute 1/4 cup oat bran for 1/4 cup bread crumbs.

Preheat oven to 400F (205C). Rinse chicken and pat dry. Place bread crumbs and seasonings in a plastic bag; shake to mix. Add oil and shake again. Put chicken in bag 1 piece at a time and shake until well-coated. Place in a medium-size shallow baking dish. Bake, uncovered, 1 hour or until tender. Serve immediately.

Yield: 4 servings

1 serving contains:

Cal	Prot	Fat	Chol	Carb	Fib	Sodium
272kc	30gm	8gm	73mg	19gm	0	248mg

Good & Simple Baked Chicken

Tender chicken breasts in a mild tarragon sauce.

2 chicken breasts, halved, skinned

1 teaspoon melted low-fat margarine

1/2 cup white wine

1/4 teaspoon dried-leaf tarragon

1/2 teaspoon onion powder

Salt and pepper to taste

2 teaspoons cornstarch

2 tablespoons water

Preheat oven to 350F (175C). Rinse chicken and pat dry. Place in a medium-size shallow baking dish. In a small bowl, blend margarine, wine, tarragon, onion powder, salt and pepper; pour over chicken. Bake, uncovered, 1 hour or until tender, basting occasionally with juices. Pour juices from cooked chicken into a pan; set over medium heat. Blend cornstarch with water. Add to juices, stirring constantly until thickened. Spoon over chicken and serve.

Yield: 4 servings

1 serving contains:

Cal	Prot	Fat	Chol	Carb	Fib	Sodium
172kc	27gm	4gm	73mg	2gm	0	137mg

Lemony-Ginger Chicken

Low-fat variation of an old favorite.

1 chicken breast, halved, skinned

1/3 cup lemon juice

1 garlic clove, minced

1/2 teaspoon minced fresh ginger root

2 tablespoons all-purpose flour

1/4 teaspoon ground ginger

Salt and pepper to taste

1 teaspoon olive oil

1 tablespoon water

1 teaspoon brown sugar

2 thin lemon slices

Rinse chicken and pat dry. Place in a small, shallow dish. In a small bowl, combine lemon juice, garlic and fresh ginger; pour over chicken. Cover and refrigerate at least 1 hour. Preheat oven to 350F (175C). Remove chicken from marinade and dry with paper towel; reserve marinade. Combine flour, ground ginger, salt and pepper in a plastic bag. Put chicken in flour mixture; shake gently to coat. Heat oil in a non-stick skillet over medium heat. Cook chicken in oil until brown on both sides. Place chicken in a small, shallow baking dish. Combine 2 tablespoons reserved marinade and 1 tablespoon water; pour over chicken. Spoon brown sugar on top of chicken pieces; place a lemon slice on top of sugar. Bake, uncovered, 45 minutes to 1 hour or until tender. Serve immediately.

Yield: 2 servings

1 serving contains:

Cal	Prot	Fat	Chol	Carb	Fib	Sodium
214kc	28gm	5gm	73mg	14gm	trace	65mg

Chicken & Broccoli Casserole

Colorful and delicious.

2 tablespoons all-purpose flour

2 tablespoons cornstarch

2 tablespoons non-fat powdered milk

1 teaspoon chicken bouillon granules

2-1/2 cups skim milk

Salt and white pepper to taste

6 cups trimmed fresh broccoli or 2 (10-oz.) pkgs. frozen spears or asparagus

2 cups cooked chicken, cut in bite-size pieces

3/4 cup low-fat mayonnaise-type salad dressing

1 teaspoon lemon juice

1/2 teaspoon curry powder

1/2 cup shredded low-fat cheddar cheese

1/2 cup fresh bread crumbs

2 tablespoons oat bran

Preheat oven to 350F (175C). In a saucepan, combine flour, cornstarch, powdered milk and bouillon granules. Slowly add skim milk, stirring well to blend. Cook over medium heat until sauce thickens, stirring constantly. Add salt and pepper; set aside. Steam broccoli until just tender; drain well. Arrange in a shallow baking dish; lay chicken on top of broccoli. Stir salad dressing, lemon juice and curry powder in white sauce; pour over chicken. Sprinkle cheese over all. Combine bread crumbs and oat bran, then sprinkle on top of cheese. Bake uncovered, 25 to 30 minutes or until bubbling and brown. Serve immediately.

Yield: 6 servings

1 serving contains:

Cal	Prot	Fat	Chol	Carb	Fib	Sodium
265kc	24gm	8gm	49gm	27gm	4gm	377mg

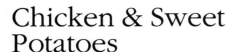

Chicken & Sweet Potatoes

A ring of sweet potatoes surrounds a chicken filling.

2 cups mashed, cooked sweet potatoes

2 tablespoons brown sugar

1/2 teaspoon ground cinnamon

1/8 teaspoon ground nutmeg

1/3 cup skimmed evaporated milk

1/4 cup chicken broth

1/4 cup minced onion

1 (8-oz.) can water chestnuts, drained, sliced

1 (10-3/4-oz.) can cream of chicken soup or Basic White Sauce with chicken flavoring, page 236

3 cups cubed cooked chicken

3 tablespoons water

Preheat oven to 350F (175C). In a medium-size bowl, combine sweet potatoes, brown sugar, cinnamon, nutmeg and milk. Spread around the inside edge of a round 10-inch casserole, forming a ring. In a medium-size non-stick skillet, heat broth over low heat. Add onion and water chestnuts; cook until tender. Add soup or sauce, chicken and 3 tablespoons water; cook over medium heat until hot, stirring occasionally. Spoon chicken mixture into center of sweet-potato ring in casserole. Bake uncovered, 30 minutes or until bubbling. Serve immediately.

Yield: 6 (1-1/4-cup) servings

1 serving contains:

Cal	Prot	Fat	Chol	Carb	Fib	Sodium
308kc	23gm	6gm	53mg	42gm	2gm	510mg

Chicken & Vegetable Casserole

A great make-ahead one-dish meal.

2 chicken breasts, halved, skinned

4 carrots, scraped, quartered

1 cup pearl onions

2 celery stalks, cut in large pieces, about 1-1/2 cups

2 potatoes, peeled, cut into quarters, about 2 cups

1/4 cup chicken broth

1 (10-3/4-oz.) can cream of mushroom soup, or Basic White Sauce with chicken flavoring, page 236

1/2 cup skim milk

1/4 teaspoon dried-leaf thyme

1/8 teaspoon ground sage

1 bay leaf

Preheat oven to 350F (175C). Rinse chicken and pat dry. Heat a medium-size non-stick skillet over low heat; spray lightly with vegetable spray. Add chicken and cook quickly until browned on both sides. Remove chicken to a medium-size shallow casserole. Add vegetables to casserole. In a small bowl, combine broth, soup or sauce, milk, thyme, sage and bay leaf; pour over chicken and vegetables. Cover and refrigerate until ready to bake. Bake, covered, 1 hour or until vegetables and chicken are tender. Serve immediately.

Yield: 4 servings

1 serving contains:

Cal	Prot	Fat	Chol	Carb	Fib	Sodium
343kc	32gm	9gm	75mg	32gm	4gm	803mg

Chicken au Gratin Casserole

Tender chicken in a creamy cheese sauce.

1/4 cup chicken broth

1/4 cup all-purpose flour

1 tablespoon non-fat powdered milk

2 cups skim milk

1/2 cup shredded low-fat cheddar cheese

3-1/2 cups cubed cooked chicken

Pepper to taste

1/2 cup fresh bread crumbs

Variation

Substitute 2 tablespoons oat bran for 2 tablespoons bread crumbs; add salt to taste.
Slice a few mushrooms and add with the cheese for a flavorful sauce.

Preheat oven to 350F (175C). Heat broth in medium-size saucepan over medium heat. In a jar with a lid, combine flour, powdered milk and skim milk; shake well to dissolve. Slowly add milk mixture to broth, stirring constantly until sauce thickens. Add cheese and stir until melted. Gently stir in chicken; season with pepper. Spoon into a medium-size shallow baking dish. Sprinkle bread crumbs over all. Bake, uncovered, 40 minutes or until bubbling. Serve immediately.

Yield: 6 servings

1 serving contains:

Cal	Prot	Fat	Chol	Carb	Fib	Sodium
206kc	25gm	4gm	57mg	15gm	trace	250mg

Chicken in Wine Sauce

A simple and delicious one-dish meal.

1 cup uncooked long-grain rice

1/2 envelope onion-soup mix

1 (10-3/4-oz.) can mushroom soup or Basic White Sauce with mushrooms, page 236

1-1/2 cups boiling water

1/4 cup white wine

2 tablespoons pimiento

2 chicken breasts, halved, skinned

1/4 teaspoon paprika

Pepper to taste

Preheat oven to 350F (175C). In a large bowl, combine rice, onion-soup mix, mushroom soup or sauce, water, wine and pimiento. Pour into a large casserole. Rinse chicken and pat dry. Arrange on top of rice mixture. Sprinkle with paprika and pepper. Bake, covered, 1 hour or until tender and liquid is absorbed. Serve immediately.

Yield: 4 servings

1 serving contains:

Cal	Prot	Fat	Chol	Carb	Fib	Sodium
362kc	31gm	9gm	75mg	34gm	2gm	1133mg

Honey-Grilled Chicken

Chicken with an intriguing sweet-tart flavor.

2 chicken breasts, halved, skinned

1/4 cup brown mustard

1/2 cup honey

1 teaspoon curry powder

Variation

Place 4 fresh peach halves on grill for the final 10 minutes of cooking. Cook until tender, basting frequently with the marinade.

Rinse chicken and pat dry. Place chicken in a medium-size shallow baking dish. In a small saucepan, blend mustard, honey and curry powder. Stir until warm over low heat; pour over chicken. Cover and marinate in refrigerator at least 1 hour. Remove chicken from marinade, reserving marinade. Place chicken on a hot grill 3 to 4 inches from coals. Cook 30 to 40 minutes until tender, turning and brushing occasionally with marinade. Serve immediately.

Yield: 4 servings

1 serving contains:

Cal	Prot	Fat	Chol	Carb	Fib	Sodium
288kc	28gm	4gm	73mg	35gm	0	270mg

Grilled Chicken with Herbs

A great low-sodium recipe.

1 garlic clove, minced

2 tablespoons oil of choice

1 teaspoon dried-leaf rosemary

1/2 teaspoon pepper

1 teaspoon ground sage

1/4 cup lemon juice

2 chicken breasts, halved, skinned

In a small bowl, combine garlic, oil, rosemary, pepper, sage and lemon juice. Rinse chicken and pat dry. Arrange in a medium-size shallow baking dish; pour oil mixture over chicken. Cover and marinate in refrigerator 3 to 4 hours. Remove chicken from marinade, reserving marinade. Place chicken on a hot grill 3 to 4 inches from coals. Cook 30 to 40 minutes or until tender, turning and brushing occasionally with marinade. Serve immediately.

Yield: 4 servings

1 serving contains:

Cal	Prot	Fat	Chol	Carb	Fib	Sodium
209kc	27gm	10gm	73mg	2gm	trace	64mg

Grilled Cornish Hens

Serve with Macaroni Salad, page 105, for a patio dinner.

2 Cornish hens, split through the breast

1/2 cup no-oil Italian salad dressing

1/2 cup Grandma's Barbecue Sauce, page 234

Heat grill. Lay Cornish hens flat on grill 3 to 4 inches from coals. Cook 40 to 50 minutes, turning and basting occasionally with Italian salad dressing. When hens are almost done, baste frequently with Barbecue Sauce, turning often until tender. Serve immediately.

Yield: 2 servings

1 serving contains:

Cal	Prot	Fat	Chol	Carb	Fib	Sodium
513kc	60gm	22gm	170mg	18gm	1gm	1087mg

Sweet & Sour Grilled Chicken

An interesting combination of flavors.

2 chicken breasts, halved, skinned

1/3 cup honey

1/3 cup lemon juice

2 tablespoons Worcestershire sauce

3 tablespoons brown mustard

1/2 cup white wine

1/4 teaspoon dried-leaf basil, crushed

1/4 teaspoon red-pepper sauce

Rinse chicken and pat dry. Place in a medium-size shallow dish. In a small saucepan, blend honey, lemon juice, Worcestershire sauce, mustard, wine, basil and red-pepper sauce. Stir until warm over low heat; pour over chicken. Cover and marinate in refrigerater at least 1 hour. Remove chicken from marinade, reserving marinade. Place chicken on a hot grill 3 to 4 inches from coals. Cook 30 to 40 minutes or until tender, turning and brushing occasionally with marinade. Serve immediately.

Yield: 4 servings

1 serving contains:

Cal	Prot	Fat	Chol	Carb	Fib	Sodium
269kc	28gm	4gm	73mg	26gm	trace	294mg

Chicken Tetrazzini

Terrific with green salad.

1 cup sliced fresh mushrooms

1/2 cup chopped onion

1-2/3 cups chicken broth

2 tablespoons all-purpose flour

1 cup skimmed evaporated milk

1/4 cup white wine

1/2 teaspoon salt

Pepper to taste

1/2 cup grated Parmesan cheese

6 oz. spaghetti

1-1/2 cups diced cooked chicken

Preheat oven to 350F (175C). In a large non-stick skillet over low heat, cook mushrooms and onion in 2 tablespoons chicken broth until tender. Remove from skillet; set aside. In a jar with a lid, combine flour, remaining chicken broth and evaporated milk; shake until completely dissolved. Add to skillet and cook over medium heat, stirring constantly until thickened. Remove from heat and stir in wine, salt, pepper and 1/4 cup Parmesan cheese; set aside. While preparing sauce, cook spaghetti according to package directions; drain well. Combine spaghetti, mushrooms, onion and chicken in a medium-size shallow baking dish. Pour sauce over all and sprinkle with remaining cheese. Bake, uncovered, 25 minutes or until bubbling. Serve immediately.

Yield: 4 servings

1 serving contains:

Cal	Prot	Fat	Chol	Carb	Fib	Sodium
411kc	37gm	7gm	68mg	38gm	1gm	727mg

Pasta with Chicken

Chicken cubes are a delightful surprise.

1/2 cup chopped onion

1/2 cup chopped green bell pepper

1/4 cup water

1/2 cup sliced fresh mushrooms

2 cups Marinara Sauce, page 237, or spaghetti sauce of choice

1-1/2 boneless chicken breasts, halved, skinned, cut into small cubes

1 tablespoon all-purpose flour

1/4 teaspoon salt

Pepper to taste

2 teaspoons olive oil

1 garlic clove, minced

8 oz. spaghetti or pasta of choice

In a large non-stick skillet over low heat, cook onion and green pepper in water until tender. Add mushrooms and stir briskly about 2 minutes. Stir in spaghetti sauce and simmer at least 30 minutes. While sauce is cooking, dredge chicken in flour, salt and pepper. In another large non-stick skillet over medium-high heat, heat 1/2 teaspoon oil and garlic about 5 seconds, stirring briskly; transfer garlic to sauce. Add remaining oil to skillet; add chicken and stir-fry over medium-high heat until chicken is tender. In a large kettle, cook pasta according to package directions. Ten minutes before serving, add chicken to sauce and simmer just until heated through. Arrange pasta on a large platter and spoon sauce with chicken over all. Serve immediately.

Yield: 6 servings

1 serving contains:

Cal	Prot	Fat	Chol	Carb	Fib	Sodium
299kc	20gm	8gm	37mg	39gm	1gm	527mg

Spaghetti Trivigno

A great Italian-style meal that's quick to prepare.

2 boneless chicken breasts, halved, skinned

5 tablespoons all-purpose flour

1/4 teaspoon salt

Pepper to taste

1 tablespoon olive oil

2 garlic cloves, minced

1/2 cup chopped onion

1 cup sliced fresh mushrooms

1/2 cup white wine

2 cups chicken broth

1/4 cup frozen peas

8 oz. spaghetti

2 egg whites, slightly beaten

2 tablespoons chopped fresh parsley, to garnish

1/3 cup grated Parmesan cheese

Rinse chicken and pat dry. Pound until thin; cut into narrow strips. Dredge chicken with flour, salt and pepper; set aside. Heat 1 teaspoon oil in a large non-stick skillet over medium-low heat. Add garlic, onion and mushrooms; sauté until tender, then set aside. Heat remaining oil in skillet over medium heat. Add chicken strips and stir-fry quickly until browned; set aside. Reduce heat. In a jar with a lid, combine remaining flour, wine and chicken broth; shake well. Slowly pour into skillet, stirring constantly until mixture begins to thicken. Add peas and simmer 10 minutes. Add chicken-and-onion mixture. Cook spaghetti according to package directions; drain well. Put spaghetti in a large pasta bowl, spoon sauce over and toss gently. Add egg whites and toss gently. Sprinkle with parsley. Serve immediately with Parmesan cheese.

Yield: 5 servings

1 serving contains:

Cal	Prot	Fat	Chol	Carb	Fib	Sodium
382kc	34gm	9gm	64mg	38gm	2gm	590mg

Chicken-Stuffed Pasta Shells

A good dish for company; make it early in the day.

10 to 12 large pasta shells, cooked

Filling:
1-1/2 cups finely shredded cooked chicken

2 tablespoons minced fresh parsley

1 egg white, slightly beaten

1 cup low-fat cottage cheese

2 tablespoons finely chopped pimiento

Salt and pepper to taste

Sauce:
1/4 cup chopped green onion

1-1/3 cups chicken broth

2 tablespoons all-purpose flour

1 tablespoon cornstarch

1/4 cup skimmed evaporated milk

1/4 cup white wine

1/2 cup shredded low-fat cheddar cheese

Salt and white pepper to taste

2 tablespoons grated Parmesan cheese

Lightly spray a 13" x 9" baking dish with vegetable spray. In a large bowl, combine chicken, parsley, egg white, cottage cheese, pimiento, salt and pepper; mix well. Using a teaspoon, stuff shells with mixture. Place stuffed shells in prepared baking dish. Preheat oven to 350F (175C). In saucepan, cook green onion in 2 tablespoons broth until tender. In a jar with a lid, combine flour, cornstarch and 1/2 cup broth; shake until dissolved. Add to onion in saucepan. Cook, stirring constantly, until mixture starts to boil and thicken; cook 1 minute longer. Gradually add remaining broth, milk, wine and cheese, stirring until cheese is melted. Remove from heat and add salt and pepper. Spoon sauce over shells; sprinkle with Parmesan cheese. Bake, uncovered, 30 minutes or until bubbling. Serve immediately.

Yield: 10 (1-shell) servings

1 serving contains:

Cal	Prot	Fat	Chol	Carb	Fib	Sodium
172kc	18gm	4gm	32mg	14gm	trace	370mg

Chicken Chili

Our favorite chili. Corn Bread, page 72, rounds it out perfectly. I keep a batch in my freezer.

1 boneless chicken breast, skinned

1/2 cup coarsely chopped green bell pepper

1/2 cup coarsely chopped onion

3/4 cup water

3 tablespoons chili-seasoning mix

8 oz. tomato sauce

1/4 cup chopped canned green chilies

1-1/2 cups cooked kidney beans

1-1/2 cups cooked pinto beans

Chop chicken into very small pieces; set aside. In a large non-stick skillet over low heat, cook green pepper and onion in 2 tablespoons water until tender; remove from skillet and set aside. Add chicken and 2 tablespoons water to skillet; cook until tender. Add seasoning mix and stir well. Stir in tomato sauce, green chilies, beans, green peppers, onion and 1/2 cup water. Simmer about 30 minutes, stirring occasionally. Serve immediately.

Yield: 6 servings

1 serving contains:

Cal	Prot	Fat	Chol	Carb	Fib	Sodium
222kc	19gm	2gm	24mg	33gm	6gm	300mg

Southwest Chicken Enchiladas

Serve with Margaritas and homemade Corn Chips, page 40. Shredded lettuce and Refried Beans, page 202, are natural accompaniments.

2 cups shredded, cooked chicken

1/2 cup tomatoes, chopped small but not fine

1/4 cup chopped canned green chilies

1/4 teaspoon ground chili powder

1/3 cup chopped onion

1 cup (4 oz.) shredded low-fat cheddar cheese

4 cups salsa

10 small flour tortillas

Preheat oven to 350F (175C). In a medium-size bowl, combine chicken, tomatoes, chilies, chili powder, onion and 1/2 cup cheese. Add about 3/4 cup salsa; mix well. Pour remaining salsa in a shallow, wide dish. Dip a tortilla in salsa and lay on a plate. Place about 1/3 cup chicken mixture in a strip toward one side of tortilla; roll up and place in a 13" x 9" casserole. Repeat with remaining tortillas and chicken mixture. Pour remaining salsa over filled enchiladas; sprinkle remaining cheese over all. Bake, covered, 30 minutes. Serve immediately.

Yield: 5 (2-enchilada) servings

1 serving contains:

Cal	Prot	Fat	Chol	Carb	Fib	Sodium
416kc	31gm	14gm	60mg	51gm	1gm	920mg

Chicken Fajitas

*A fun meal, great for a casual dinner.
Serve Refried Beans, page 202, on the
side.*

**2 boneless chicken breasts, halved,
skinned**

1 cup no-oil Italian salad dressing

1-1/2 cups salsa

1 teaspoon oil of choice

1 garlic clove, minced

1 cup coarsely chopped onion

**1 cup coarsely chopped green bell
pepper**

Dash of ground cumin

Pepper to taste

**1 medium-size tomato, cut into
small wedges**

1/2 cup plain low-fat yogurt

8 flour tortillas, warmed

Rinse chicken and pat dry. In a medium-
size dish, combine salad dressing and 1
cup salsa. Add chicken; turn until
coated. Cover and refrigerate at least 2
hours. Heat charcoal grill. Place chicken
on grill 3 to 4 inches from coals. Cook
until tender, turning and basting occasionally with marinade. Remove from
grill; set aside. In a large non-stick skillet, heat oil over medium heat. Add garlic, onion and green pepper; sauté until
tender. Stir in cumin and pepper. Slice
chicken into finger-size pieces. When
vegetables are tender, add chicken
pieces and toss together; spoon into a
serving dish. To serve, take 1 tortilla and
spoon 3 tablespoons chicken mixture
into center of tortilla, leaving the bottom
free. Add tomato wedges, about 1 tablespoon yogurt and salsa to taste. Fold
bottom of tortilla up, then fold each side
in toward center making a filled pocket.

Yield: 4 (2-fajita) servings

1 serving contains:

Cal	Prot	Fat	Chol	Carb	Fib	Sodium
441kc	35gm	10gm	75mg	57gm	1gm	791mg

Ground-Turkey Taco Filling

For a Mexican treat, serve with Spanish Lima Beans, page 197, or steamed rice.

1 lb. raw ground turkey

1/3 cup chopped onion

2 tablespoons all-purpose flour

1/2 teaspoon ground cumin

Salt to taste

8 oz. tomato sauce

12 taco or tostada shells (made with acceptable oil)

Toppings:

Shredded lettuce

Shredded low-fat cheese

Salsa

Chopped green onion

Sliced radishes

In a large non-stick skillet over medium-low heat, sauté ground turkey until almost done; add onion and cook until tender. Quickly stir in flour, blending well. Stir in cumin and salt, then tomato sauce. Simmer over low heat at least 10 minutes. Fill taco or tostada shells and garnish as desired.

Yield: (2-taco) servings

1 serving contains:

Cal	Prot	Fat	Chol	Carb	Fib	Sodium
253kc	25gm	8gm	58mg	20gm	trace	301mg

Audrey's Oriental Chicken

Serve this when you want something delicious and different for company dinner. Serve with plain boiled rice.

1/4 cup firmly packed brown sugar

2 tablespoons cornstarch

1/4 cup vinegar

1 tablespoon soy sauce

1 (15-oz.) can pineapple chunks, packed in natural juice

1 cup strips green bell pepper

1 cup thin onion rings

1 tablespoon oil of choice

2 boneless chicken breasts, skinned, cut into thin strips

In a medium-size bowl, combine sugar and cornstarch. Gradually stir in vinegar and soy sauce. Stir in pineapple, green pepper and onion; set aside. Heat oil in a wok or large non-stick skillet over medium-high heat. Add chicken and stir-fry quickly, just until tender and chicken has turned white. Add pineapple and vegetable mixture; stir until well-mixed. Cover and simmer over low heat 15 minutes. Serve immediately.

Yield: 4 (1-1/4-cup) servings

1 serving contains:

Cal	Prot	Fat	Chol	Carb	Fib	Sodium
314kc	28gm	7gm	73mg	36gm	2gm	327mg

Johnny's Pot Pie

Our son's hearty wintertime favorite.

2 carrots, chopped

1 onion, chopped

1/2 cup chopped celery

1 cup baby lima beans

1/2 teaspoon dried-leaf thyme

2 small potatoes, chopped

1 cup frozen peas

1/4 cup all-purpose flour

1-1/2 cups skim milk

2 tablespoons non-fat powdered milk

About 1/2 teaspoon salt

1/4 teaspoon pepper

2 to 3 cups chopped cooked chicken

1-1/4 cups Baking Mix, page 65

2 tablespoons low-fat margarine, room temperature

5 tablespoons very hot water

In a large saucepan, cook carrots, onion, celery, limas and thyme in boiling water for 10 minutes. Add potatoes and cook until tender; add peas and cook until tender; drain well. In a jar with a lid, combine flour, 1 cup milk and powdered milk; shake until completely dissolved. Pour into a saucepan, stirring constantly over medium heat. Add salt and pepper; stir constantly until thickened. Stir in 1/2 cup milk and chicken. Stir vegetables into chicken mixture; mix well. Pour into a 9-inch-square baking dish. Preheat oven to 450C (230C). In a bowl, combine Baking Mix and margarine; add hot water and stir until dough forms a soft ball. With floured hands, flatten dough into a 9-inch square. Gently roll up dough and place on top of chicken mixture. Unroll to fit dish. Bake about 8 minutes or until browned. Let pie stand a few minutes before serving.

Yield: 6 servings

1 serving contains:

Cal	Prot	Fat	Chol	Carb	Fib	Sodium
357kc	28gm	7gm	50mg	45gm	5gm	505mg

Chicken Dinner in a Pot

A perfect Sunday meal to cook in the oven while at church. Serve Homemade Biscuits, page 66, on the side for a Southern touch.

1 (5- to 6-lb.) roasting chicken

Salt to taste, optional

1/2 cup white wine

1/4 teaspoon dried-leaf rosemary

1 small bay leaf

1/2 cup chopped celery

1 medium onion, cut into wedges

6 carrots, peeled, cut into pieces

6 potatoes, peeled, quartered

Preheat oven to 350F (175C). Rinse chicken inside and out; pat dry. Rub inside of chicken with salt, if desired; place in a roasting pan. Add wine, rosemary and bay leaf. Bake, covered, about 45 minutes. Add celery, onion and carrots; cook about 30 minutes longer. Add potatoes and cook 2 hours longer or until everything is tender. Serve immediately.

Yield: 6 servings

1 serving contains:

Cal	Prot	Fat	Chol ,	Carb	Fib	Sodium
306kc	28gm	5gm	73mg	33gm	3gm	95mg

Curried Chicken

Curry enhances the flavor of baked chicken. Accompany with fresh fruit and a plain rice dish.

3 chicken breasts, halved, skinned

3 tablespoons all-purpose flour

1-1/2 cups sliced onion

1 tablespoon water

1 apple, peeled, chopped

1/4 teaspoon curry powder

1/8 teaspoon ground ginger

1/8 teaspoon ground tumeric

1/2 teaspoon salt

1/8 teaspoon pepper

1 cup chicken broth

1/3 cup raisins

Preheat oven to 350F (175C). Rinse chicken and pat dry; dredge in flour. Spray a large non-stick skillet with vegetable spray; heat over medium high. Add chicken and cook just until brown; turn and brown other side. Put chicken in a medium-size shallow casserole. In skillet over low heat, cook onion in 1 tablespoon water 5 minutes; add apple and cook 1 minute. Spoon over chicken; sprinkle with spices. Pour broth over all. Bake, covered, 55 minutes or until tender. Add raisins and cook 5 minutes longer. Serve immediately.

Yield: 6 servings

1 serving contains:

Cal	Prot	Fat	Chol	Carb	Fib	Sodium
214kc	29gm	4gm	73mg	16gm	2gm	357mg

Turkey Loaf

Serve hot with potatoes and Coleslaw, page 94. Slice the cold leftovers for delicious sandwiches.

About 3/4 cup coarsely crushed Wheaties® or Cornflakes®

1/4 cup oat bran or 1/4 cup cereal crumbs

3/4 cup milk

2 egg whites

1/4 cup chopped onion

1/4 cup chopped green bell pepper

1/2 teaspoon ground sage

1/2 teaspoon salt

1/8 teaspoon pepper

1 teaspoon parsley flakes

1 lb. raw ground turkey

2 tablespoons brown sugar

1/4 cup catsup

1 teaspoon dry mustard

1/4 teaspoon ground nutmeg

1/8 teaspoon ground ginger

In a large bowl, combine cereal crumbs, oat bran, milk, egg whites, onion, green pepper, sage, salt, pepper and parsley; mix well. Add ground turkey and blend thoroughly. Turkey mixture should be firm enough to shape; if not, add more cereal crumbs. Spoon mixture into a shallow 2-quart casserole and form into a dome shape or press into a 9" x 5" loaf pan; set aside. In a small bowl, combine brown sugar, catsup, mustard, nutmeg and ginger; pour over loaf. Bake, uncovered, 1 hour. Serve immediately.

Yield: 6 servings

1 serving contains:

Cal	Prot	Fat	Chol	Carb	Fib	Sodium
166kc	20gm	3gm	49mg	15gm	1	390mg

Stir-Fried Chicken & Vegetables

A quick, easy dish if you prepare the vegetables ahead. Serve with plain boiled rice.

2 tablespoons cornstarch

1/2 cup chicken broth

2 tablespoons soy sauce

1/4 cup light corn syrup

1 tablespoon plus 1 teaspoon corn oil

1 garlic clove, minced

1 thin slice fresh ginger root

4 cups vegetables, cut for stir-frying

1-1/2 boneless chicken breasts, skinned, cut into thin strips

In a small bowl, combine cornstarch and broth. Stir in soy sauce and corn syrup; set aside. In a large wok or non-stick skillet, heat 1 tablespoon oil; add garlic and ginger root, stirring about 5 seconds, then add vegetables. Stir-fry quickly about 1 minute to coat with oil, then reduce heat and cook about 3 minutes longer. Remove from skillet. Heat remaining oil in skillet; add chicken and stir-fry until chicken becomes white and is tender. Return vegetables to skillet. Stir cornstarch mixture, then add to skillet, stirring constantly. Bring to a boil. Cook 30 seconds or until sauce thickens. Serve immediately.

Yield: 4 servings

1 serving contains:

Cal	Prot	Fat	Chol	Carb	Fib	Sodium
261kc	22gm	8gm	55mg	25gm	2gm	173mg

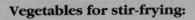

Vegetables for stir-frying:

Green, red or yellow bell peppers,
    cut into medium-size slices
Broccoli, cut into flowerets
Carrot, thinly sliced
Cauliflower, cut into flowerets
Mushrooms, thickly sliced
Onion, thinly sliced
Snow peas, whole
Water chestnuts, medium sliced

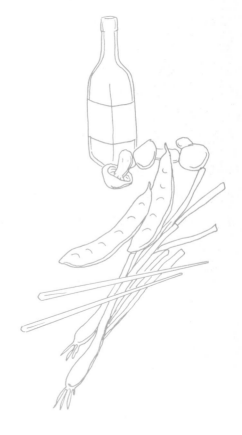

Stuffed Peppers

A great meal to make ahead and freeze.

4 medium-size green bell peppers, tops and seeds removed, washed

1/2 cup chopped onion

2 tablespoons water

8 oz. raw ground turkey

3/4 cup cooked rice

1/4 teaspoon salt

1/8 teaspoon black pepper

1/8 teaspoon garlic powder

1 teaspoon Worcestershire sauce

1 (10-1/2-oz.) can tomato soup

Preheat oven to 350F (175C). Bring a large saucepan filled with water to a boil; add green peppers and return to a boil. Reduce heat to medium and cook 5 minutes. Remove from water and drain upside down on paper towel. In a large non-stick skillet over medium-low heat, cook onion in 2 tablespoons water. Add ground turkey and cook, stirring occasionally, until turkey loses its pink color. Add rice, salt, black pepper, garlic powder, Worcestershire sauce and 1/2 can tomato soup. Stir until well-blended. Using a large spoon, fill green peppers with turkey mixture. Set upright in a 9" x 5" loaf pan. Spoon remaining soup over top of peppers. Bake, uncovered, 30 minutes. Serve immediately.

Yield: 4 servings

1 serving contains:

Cal	Prot	Fat	Chol	Carb	Fib	Sodium
163kc	11gm	3gm	23mg	25gm	2gm	694mg

Cooked Chicken

The basis for a wide variety of dishes.

2 whole chicken breasts, halved, skinned

1 bay leaf

1 teaspoon dried-leaf thyme

1/2 teaspoon salt

1/2 onion, quartered

Rinse chicken. Place all ingredients in a large pot; add enough water to cover chicken. Simmer 45 to 50 minutes or until chicken is tender; be careful not to overcook. Cool chicken in broth. Discard onion and bay leaf. Broth can be used immediately or frozen for later use. Chicken can be chopped and used in casseroles, salads, soups or many other dishes.

Yield: 4 servings

1 serving contains:

Cal	Prot	Fat	Chol	Carb	Fib	Sodium
151kc	27gm	3gm	73mg	2gm	trace	308mg

Seafood

If fresh and prepared properly, fish is a delicious entrée. It is lower in calories, saturated fat and in most cases (except for shrimp and lobster), lower in cholesterol than beef, pork or lamb. Fish is an excellent source of protein, B vitamins and many minerals. Cold-water fish—such as salmon—is a good source of the omega-3 fatty acids, which have been shown to lower lipid levels. Aside from all the health benefits, fish is about the quickest entrée to cook and it can be prepared in many ways.

I grew up near a fresh-water lake with an avid fisherman father. We ate lots of fish, but it was always fried. I grew up thinking baked fish was for sick people. There are many people who still have this misconception. I hope my recipes will change your opinion of fish.

I highly recommend Linguine & Clam Sauce. It is one of the easiest recipes in this book, yet good enough to serve your guests. Try one of the scallop recipes—scallops are one of my favorite seafood dishes. Sautéed Scallops is simple and delicious. Brenda's Breaded Fish is a family favorite entrée. Using good quality fish, this combination results in an excellent entrée. For a different taste, try Lemon-Soy Fish Fillets. Be sure to let the fish marinate to develop the full oriental flavor. Serve with rice and steamed vegetable for a delicious, nutritious and easily prepared meal.

Frozen fish is an excellent alternative to fresh fish if it is thawed slowly in the refrigerator. As with most foods, never refreeze once it has thawed.

Fish can be prepared in a variety of ways and the basic techniques are explained at right. Be careful not to overcook fish. Serve as soon as it is ready.

To Broil Fish: Preheat broiler with oven door ajar. Lightly oil rack, unless oil is used on fish. Broil fillets 3 to 4 inches from heat source 4 to 5 minutes or until fish flakes easily. Cook thicker pieces 10 minutes per inch. Only thick pieces need to be turned.

To Grill Fish: Preheat grill. Lightly rub grill rack with oil. Grill fillets 6 to 8 minutes or until fish flakes easily. Cook directly on grill rack, in a fish-grilling basket or in foil boats.

To Poach Fish: Put poaching liquid or a combination of water, herbs and wine in a large shallow pan or skillet. Add fish and bring to a boil. Reduce heat and simmer until fish flakes easily, about 10 minutes for a 1-inch-thick piece of fish.

To Steam Fish in Foil: Lay fish in center of a large piece of heavy-duty aluminum foil. Add remaining ingredients. Fold foil over fish and seal edges tightly. Bake in preheated oven or on a grill until fish flakes easily.

So-easy Fish

Delightful recipe for a busy day.

2 fillets white fish, about 8 oz.

1/2 teaspoon oil of choice

1/4 cup fresh bread crumbs

1 teaspoon grated Parmesan cheese

1/8 teaspoon garlic powder

1/8 teaspoon lemon pepper

Variation

Substitute 1 tablespoon oat bran for
   1 tablespoon bread crumbs.

Preheat oven to 425F (220C). Rinse fish and pat dry. Lightly grease a small shallow baking pan with some of oil. Rub remaining oil over top of fish. In a small bowl, combine remaining ingredients and sprinkle over fish. Bake, uncovered, about 20 minutes or until fish flakes easily. Serve immediately.

Yield: 2 servings

1 serving contains:

Cal	Prot	Fat	Chol	Carb	Fib	Sodium
169kc	24gm	3gm	56mg	9gm	0	204mg

Baked Fish & Herbs

Serve with Brown-Rice Pilaf, page 200, and a colorful vegetable.

4 fillets white fish, about 1 lb.

2 green onions, thinly sliced

1 tablespoon chopped fresh parsley

1/4 teaspoon dried-leaf mixed Italian herbs

1/8 teaspoon lemon pepper

1 firm tomato, sliced

1/8 cup white wine

1 tablespoon lemon juice

1 tablespoon low-fat margarine, melted

Cherry tomatoes

Preheat oven to 400F (205C). Lightly spray a medium-size shallow baking pan with vegetable spray. Rinse fish and pat dry. Arrange fish in baking pan. Sprinkle green onions over fish. In a small bowl, mix together parsley, Italian herbs and lemon pepper. Sprinkle half of mixture over fish and onions. Lay tomato slices over fish and sprinkle with remaining herbs. In a small bowl, combine wine and lemon juice. Pour over fish, then drizzle margarine over all. Bake, uncovered, 15 to 20 minutes or until fish flakes easily. Garnish with cherry tomatoes. Serve immediately.

Yield: 4 servings

1 serving contains:

Cal	Prot	Fat	Chol	Carb	Fib	Sodium
133kc	22gm	3gm	55mg	4gm	1gm	131mg

Baked Fish with Tomatoes

An easy, low-calorie entrée.

2 fillets white fish, about 8 oz.

2 firm tomatoes, cut in half

1/8 teaspoon grated lemon peel

Pepper to taste

1/2 teaspoon oregano

1/2 tablespoon snipped chives

1/4 teaspoon dill weed

1 tablespoon low-fat margarine, melted

Preheat oven to 400F (205C). Lightly spray a small shallow baking pan with vegetable spray. Rinse fish and pat dry. Arrange fish in baking pan and place tomato halves around fish. Sprinkle lemon peel, pepper and herbs over fish and tomatoes; drizzle melted margarine over all. Bake, uncovered, 20 minutes or until fish flakes easily. Serve immediately.

Yield: 2 servings

1 serving contains:

Cal	Prot	Fat	Chol	Carb	Fib	Sodium
157kc	23gm	4gm	55mg	6gm	2gm	173mg

Brenda's Breaded Fish

Grandson Joseph loves fish prepared this way.

3 fillets white fish, about 12 oz.

2 cups loosely packed fresh bread crumbs

1/3 cup grated Parmesan cheese

1 egg white

1 tablespoon water

1/8 teaspoon lemon pepper

Dash of garlic powder

1 tablespoon low-fat margarine, melted

Parsley sprigs, lemon wedges to garnish

Variation

Substitute 1/2 cup oat bran for 1/2 cup bread crumbs.

Preheat oven to 375F (190C). Rinse fish and pat dry. In a small bowl, mix bread crumbs and Parmesan cheese. In another small bowl, beat egg white with water. Dip fish in egg white, then roll in crumbs to coat well. Lightly spray a medium-size shallow baking pan with vegetable spray. Arrange fish in baking pan and sprinkle with lemon pepper and garlic powder. Drizzle margarine over fish. Bake, uncovered, about 20 minutes or until fish flakes easily. If top doesn't brown nicely, put under the broiler for a few seconds. Garnish with parsley and lemon wedges. Serve immediately.

Yield: 3 servings

1 serving contains:

Cal	Prot	Fat	Chol	Carb	Fib	Sodium
256kc	30gm	8gm	63mg	15gm	1gm	514mg

Crispy Baked Fish & Herbs

You'll like crispy baked fish.

4 fillets white fish, about 1 lb.

1 egg white

1 tablespoon water

1/2 cup cornflake crumbs

1/8 teaspoon lemon pepper

2 teaspoons chopped fresh parsley

1 teaspoon low-fat margarine, melted

Variation

Substitute 2 tablespoons oat bran for 2 tablespoons cereal crumbs.

Preheat oven to 400F (205C). Lightly spray a medium-size shallow baking pan with vegetable spray. Rinse fish and pat dry. In a small bowl, beat egg white with a little water. Dip fish in egg white, then roll in crumbs. Arrange fish in baking pan. Sprinkle with lemon pepper and parsley, then drizzle margarine over all. Bake, uncovered, about 20 minutes or until fish flakes easily. Serve immediately.

Yield: 4 servings

1 serving contains:

Cal	Prot	Fat	Chol	Carb	Fib	Sodium
135kc	23gm	2gm	55mg	5gm	trace	187mg

Fish Rolls

For a lovely meal, serve with Cabbage Salad, page 100, Glazed Carrots & Zucchini, page 207, and Brown-Rice Pilaf, page 200.

4 fillets white fish, about 1 lb.

3 tablespoons finely chopped celery

3 tablespoons finely chopped green onion

2 teaspoons chopped fresh parsley

1 tablespoon chopped pimento

1/3 cup chicken broth

1/2 cup plus 1 tablespoon fresh bread crumbs

1 tablespoon low-fat margarine, melted

1/8 teaspoon grated lemon peel

Pepper to taste

Lime wedges to garnish

Preheat oven to 375F (190C). Lightly spray a shallow baking pan with vegetable spray. Rinse fish and pat dry; lay fish on a clean work surface. In a medium-size non-stick skillet over low heat, cook celery, onion, parsley and pimento in 1 tablespoon chicken broth until tender. Add remaining broth and enough bread crumbs to make a firm mixture. Divide bread mixture evenly over fish fillets; roll up each fillet and secure with a wooden pick. Arrange fish in baking pan. Drizzle margarine over all, then sprinkle with lemon peel and pepper. Bake, uncovered, about 20 minutes or until fish flakes easily. Garnish with lime wedges. Serve immediately.

Yield: 4 servings

1 serving contains:

Cal	Prot	Fat	Chol	Carb	Fib	Sodium
144kc	23gm	3gm	55mg	6gm	1gm	229mg

Lemon-Soy Fish Fillets

Soy sauce and ginger give an Oriental flavor.

2 fillets mild white fish, about 8 oz.

1 teaspoon low-fat margarine, melted

1 tablespoon soy sauce

1 tablespoon lemon juice

1/2 teaspoon Worcestershire sauce

1/2 teaspoon ground ginger

1 garlic clove, minced

1/8 teaspoon grated lemon peel

1/8 teaspoon freshly ground black pepper

1/2 tablespoon sugar

Parsley sprigs, lemon wedges to garnish

Rinse fish and pat dry; lay it in a shallow dish. In a small bowl, combine margarine, soy sauce, lemon juice, Worcestershire sauce, ginger, garlic, lemon peel, black pepper and sugar. Pour over fish and marinate 2 hours in refrigerator. Preheat broiler. Remove fish from marinade, reserving marinade. Place fish in broiling pan. Broil fish 4 to 5 minutes or until it flakes easily, basting with marinade at least twice. Garnish fish with parsley and lemon wedges. Serve immediately.

Yield: 2 servings

1 serving contains:

Cal	Prot	Fat	Chol	Carb	Fib	Sodium
139kc	23gm	2gm	55mg	7gm	trace	644mg

Linguine & Clam Sauce

An impressive dish that's quick and easy to prepare.

3 garlic cloves, minced

2 tablespoons minced onion

2 tablespoons olive oil

1 cup white wine

2 cups canned clams and juice

1/8 teaspoon white pepper

8 oz. linguine

2 tablespoons chopped fresh parsley

1/4 cup grated Parmesan cheese

In a large saucepan over medium-high heat, sauté garlic and onion in oil. Add wine. Reduce heat to low and simmer 30 minutes. Add clams with juice or fish and pepper; simmer about 10 minutes longer. While clams are simmering, cook linguine according to package directions; drain well. Put linguine in a large shallow serving bowl and spoon clam sauce over. Sprinkle with parsley. Serve immediately and pass Parmesan cheese to accompany.

Yield: 4 servings

1 serving contains:

Cal	Prot	Fat	Chol	Carb	Fib	Sodium
346kc	17gm	11gm	62mg	38gm	1gm	165mg

Crab Crepes

Impress your guests.

2 tablespoons all-purpose flour

1 tablespoon cornstarch

1-1/2 cups skim milk

2 tablespoons non-fat powdered milk

1/4 cup white wine

1/4 teaspoon lemon pepper

1/2 teaspoon salt

1/4 teaspoon dried-leaf tarragon

1/2 cup chopped fresh mushrooms

8 oz. imitation crab, chopped

1/2 cup sliced fresh mushrooms

10 Basic Crepes, page 84

3 tablespoons grated Parmesan cheese

Dash of paprika

Combine flour, cornstarch, 1 cup skim milk and powdered milk; stir until dissolved. Pour into saucepan. Add wine, lemon pepper, salt and tarragon. Stir over medium heat until mixture starts to thicken; cook 2 minutes longer, then remove from heat. Set aside 1/2 cup sauce. Add 1/2 cup chopped mushrooms and crab to remaining sauce; cook until heated through; set aside. Add 1/2 cup skim milk to reserved sauce, stir until blended; cook on low until heated; set aside. Lightly spray a small non-stick skillet with vegetable spray. Add sliced mushrooms and sauté; set aside. Preheat broiler. Lightly spray a 13" x 9" baking pan with vegetable spray. Lay out 10 crepes. Evenly distribute crab mixture, spreading along center of each crepe. Fold sides of crepes over and place in baking pan. Pour reserved sauce and milk over crepes; spoon sautéed mushrooms over sauce. Sprinkle with Parmesan cheese and paprika. Broil until light brown. Serve immediately.

Yield: 5 (2-crepe) servings

1 serving contains:

Cal	Prot	Fat	Chol	Carb	Fib	Sodium
268kc	18gm	3gm	14mg	40gm	1gm	770mg

Poached Sole

A low-fat, low-calorie entrée.

2 fillets sole, cut into serving pieces, about 8 oz.

2 cups water

1/4 cup lemon juice

1 parsley sprig or 1/2 tablespoon flakes

1/4 cup chopped onion

1 bay leaf

3 peppercorns

Parsley, lemon wedges to garnish

Dash of paprika

Rinse fish and pat dry. Put water, lemon juice, parsley, onion, bay leaf and peppercorns into a large shallow skillet. Bring to a boil and boil about 5 minutes. Gently place fish in broth. Cover and simmer 5 to 7 minutes or until fish flakes easily. Gently remove fish to a serving platter. Garnish with parsley and lemon wedges and sprinkle with paprika. Serve immediately.

Yield: 2 servings

1 serving contains:

Cal	Prot	Fat	Chol	Carb	Fib	Sodium
124kc	22gm	1gm	55mg	6gm	1gm	94mg

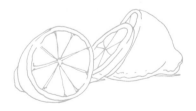

Crab Quiche

Read the label to make sure the imitation crab ingredients are allowed in your diet.

1 (9-inch) uncooked Pie Crust, page 295

2 egg whites

1/2 cup egg substitute

1/2 cup skimmed evaporated milk

1/2 cup shredded low-fat Swiss cheese

2 tablespoons chopped onion

1/4 teaspoon salt

1/4 teaspoon dried leaf marjoram

1/4 teaspoon lemon pepper

8 oz. imitation crab, cut into bite-size pieces

Preheat oven to 400F (205C). Prick pie crust and bake 4 minutes; prick again and bake 5 minutes longer. While crust is baking, combine remaining ingredients in a large bowl. Pour into pie crust and bake 30 to 40 minutes or until set. Let stand 10 minutes before serving.

Yield: 6 servings

1 serving contains:

Cal	Prot	Fat	Chol	Carb	Fib	Sodium
296kc	15gm	15gm	14mg	25gm	1gm	574mg

Salmon Patties

An old favorite with low-fat and low-cholesterol.

1 (15-1/2-oz.) can salmon

1/4 cup chopped onion

1/2 teaspoon prepared mustard

About 1 cup fine cracker crumbs

2 egg whites

1/2 cup all-purpose flour

1 teaspoon oil of choice

Variation

Substitute 1/4 cup oat bran for 1/4 cup
cracker crumbs.

Drain salmon, reserving broth. In a
large bowl, combine salmon, onion,
mustard, crumbs, egg whites, flour and
enough broth to moisten. Add more
cracker crumbs or broth if needed to
make patties firm. Flour hands and
make 4 patties; roll patties in flour. Heat
oil in a medium-size non-stick skillet
over medium heat. Add patties and
cook on both sides until browned. Serve
immediately.

Yield: 4 servings

1 serving contains:

Cal	Prot	Fat	Chol	Carb	Fib	Sodium
281kc	26gm	9gm	47mg	20gm	1gm	742mg

Sautéed Scallops

Arrange around a bed of rice.

2 teaspoons low-fat margarine

1/4 cup finely chopped celery

3 tablespoons finely chopped green onion

2 garlic cloves, minced

1-1/2 lbs. bay scallops, rinsed, drained well

3 tablespoons white wine

1/2 teaspoon dried-leaf basil

1/4 teaspoon lemon pepper

1 tablespoon chopped fresh parsley

2 tablespoons low-fat mayonnaise-type salad dressing

Melt margarine in a large non-stick skillet over medium-high heat. Add celery, green onion and garlic; sauté until wilted. Add scallops, wine, basil, lemon pepper and parsley. Cook over medium-high heat about 5 minutes or until tender, stirring often but gently. With a slotted spoon, remove scallops and vegetables to a plate. Add salad dressing to skillet, blending with scallop juices. Add scallops and toss gently to coat. Garnish with parsley. Serve immediately.

Yield: 4 (3/4-cup) servings

1 serving contains:

Cal	Prot	Fat	Chol	Carb	Fib	Sodium
177kc	29gm	3gm	57mg	6gm	trace	326mg

Sautéed Snapper

Curry powder adds a bit of color and a pleasing taste.

1 lb. red Pacific snapper

2 teaspoons low-fat margarine

2 tablespoons white wine

1 teaspoon lemon juice

1/8 teaspoon pepper

1/8 teaspoon garlic powder

Dash of curry powder

Orange slices to garnish

Rinse fish and pat dry. Cut into serving-size pieces. Melt margarine in a large non-stick skillet over medium heat. Add wine and lemon juice. Place fish in skillet; sprinkle with seasonings. Sauté a few minutes on each side until fish flakes easily. If skillet starts to get dry, add more wine. Garnish with orange slices. Serve immediately.

Yield: 4 servings

1 serving contains:

Cal	Prot	Fat	Chol	Carb	Fib	Sodium
131kc	23gm	3gm	41mg	2gm	trace	97mg

Baked Scallops with Tarragon

Looks impressive and is quick and easy to prepare.

1 cup white wine

1 tablespoon chopped fresh parsley

1/4 teaspoon dried-leaf tarragon

3 peppercorns

1 lb. bay scallops or ocean scallops, cut into quarters

1-1/2 tablespoons all-purpose flour

2 tablespoons cornstarch

2/3 cup skimmed evaporated milk

1 teaspoon lemon juice

1-1/2 tablespoons chopped pimento

1 teaspoon low-fat margarine

4 teaspoons grated Parmesan cheese

Parsley sprigs to garnish

Preheat oven to 350F (175C). In a sauce-pan, combine wine, parsley, tarragon and peppercorns. Bring to a boil; reduce heat and simmer 5 minutes. Add scallops, return to a boil. Reduce heat to medium; cook until scallops are tender and look opaque. Lift scallops from broth; set aside. In a jar with a lid, combine flour, cornstarch and milk; shake until dissolved. Gradually add to simmering broth, stirring constantly until broth thickens and starts to bubble. Cook 1 minute; add scallops, lemon juice, pimento and margarine; toss to coat well. Spoon scallops and sauce into 4 individual baking dishes or a shallow 1-quart baking dish. Sprinkle with Parmesan cheese. Bake 10 minutes or until bubbling and beginning to brown. Garnish with parsley. Serve immediately.

Yield: 4 servings

1 serving contains:

Cal	Prot	Fat	Chol	Carb	Fib	Sodium
213kc	24gm	2gm	41mg	14gm	trace	286mg

Steamed Fish in Foil

Flavorful, moist way to prepare fish.

6 fillets white fish, about 1 lb.

2 tablespoons low-fat margarine, softened

1/2 teaspoon brown mustard

1 tablespoon snipped chives

Pepper to taste

1 teaspoon lemon juice

1 small garlic clove, minced

Cilantro or parsley sprigs, lemon wedges to garnish

Preheat oven to 375F (190C). Rinse fish and pat dry. In a small bowl, blend remaining ingredients, except garnish, to a creamy mixture. Tear off a piece of heavy-duty aluminum foil large enough to wrap two pieces of fish. Lay one fillet on foil. Spread with part of creamed mixture, then cover with another fillet. Fold foil over fish and seal edges tightly. Place in a medium-size baking dish and prepare remaining fillets in the same manner. Bake 15 to 20 minutes or until fish flakes easily. Remove from foil, being careful to save juices. Garnish with cilantro or parsley and lemon wedges. Serve immediately.

Yield: 3 servings

1 serving contains:

Cal	Prot	Fat	Chol	Carb	Fib	Sodium
178kc	29gm	6gm	73mg	2gm	trace	228mg

Tuna Divan

Colorful, inexpensive one-dish meal.
Garnish with chopped pimiento.

1/2 bunch broccoli, about 8 oz.

1 cup sliced fresh mushrooms

1 (6-1/2-oz.) can white tuna, packed in water, drained

1/2 cup low-fat cottage cheese

2 cups cooked long-grain rice

1 recipe Mornay Sauce, page 238

1 cup fresh bread crumbs

1 tablespoon grated Parmesan cheese

Wash broccoli and trim off lower stalk. Cut remaining broccoli into spears. Place in a shallow 2-quart baking dish. Cook in a microwave according to directions until tender; drain and set aside. Lightly spray a small non-stick skillet with vegetable spray. Add mushrooms and sauté over medium heat until tender; set aside. In a bowl, flake tuna. Add cottage cheese, rice, Mornay sauce and mushrooms; stir gently until mixed. Spoon tuna mixture over broccoli. Sprinkle with bread crumbs and Parmesan cheese. Microwave 8 minutes on HIGH or adjust according to your own microwave. Serve immediately.

Yield: 4 (1-1/2-cup) servings

If you do not have a microwave, steam broccoli in a steamer. When casserole is ready to bake, bake in a 350F (175C) oven 25 minutes.

1 serving contains:

Cal	Prot	Fat	Chol	Carb	Fib	Sodium
389kc	30gm	5gm	25mg	55gm	4gm	796mg

Grilled Salmon

Serve with fresh corn cooked on the grill. Top the salmon with Cucuumber Sauce, page 231.

2 salmon steaks, about 1 lb.

1 teaspoon low-fat margarine, melted

1 teaspoon lemon juice

1/4 teaspoon dill weed

1/4 teaspoon garlic powder

1/4 teaspoon lemon pepper

Rinse fish and pat dry. In a small bowl, combine margarine, lemon juice, dill, garlic powder and lemon pepper. Place salmon in a shallow dish and pour margarine mixture over salmon; refrigerate at least 30 minutes. Heat a grill or broiler. Lightly brush grill rack with oil. Place salmon on grill rack 4 to 5 inches from source of heat. Cook 4 to 5 minutes, basting occasionally with juices. Turn steaks and continue basting until fish flakes easily about 4 minutes, depending on thickness of steaks. Serve immediately.

Yield: 2 servings

1 serving contains:

Cal	Prot	Fat	Chol	Carb	Fib	Sodium
289kc	43gm	14gm	77mg	1gm	0	116mg

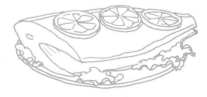

Meatless Meals

On days when your family feels like a change from poultry and seafood, feed them meatless combination dishes. They contribute nutrition and color to your menu without high fat and cholesterol.

One very important factor in serving meatless meals is to be aware of *complete* or *incomplete proteins.* Our main sources of vegetable protein are legumes (beans) and grains. Vegetable proteins are incomplete proteins, but they can be combined in a meal or in a recipe to provide a complete protein. A rule of thumb for combining these is to use twice the amount of grain as legumes. This ratio provides complete protein, plenty of fiber, vitamins and minerals with far less fat than most protein from animal sources.

In this section you will find two of our favorite meatless meals, Eggplant Mozzarella and Vegetarian Pizza. There is no end to the vegetable combinations you can use to top this delicious homemade pizza crust. Try something new each time you make it. Keep your family interested in their "no red meat" diet! Another favorite of ours is spaghetti (egg-yolk-free) and meatless spaghetti sauce, served with grated Parmesan Cheese.

Bean Enchiladas

Try a mild variety of picante sauce the first time you make this dish.

1 recipe Refried Beans, page 203, omit cheese

2 oz. diced canned green chilies

4 cups picante sauce

10 large flour tortillas

1 cup shredded low-fat cheddar cheese

Garnish Suggestions:

Shredded lettuce
Chopped green onion
Diced tomatoes
Picante sauce

Preheat oven to 350F (175C). In a large iron skillet or heavy saucepan, stir beans and green chilies over low heat until warm. Pour 1/4 cup picante sauce into a large shallow dish. Dip a tortilla in sauce, coating both sides. Remove to a plate. Spoon 1/4 to 1/3 cup of beans at 1 edge of tortilla; sprinkle a little cheese over beans and fold over. Pour 1/4 cup picante sauce in the bottom of a large shallow casserole and lay enchiladas in sauce as you make them. When all enchiladas are made, pour remaining picante sauce over all. Bake, covered, 30 minutes. Uncover, sprinkle remaining cheese on top and bake 5 minutes longer. Serve immediately garnished as desired.

Yield: 5 (2-enchilada) servings

1 serving contains:

Cal	Prot	Fat	Chol	Carb	Fib	Sodium
709kc	35gm	12gm	16mg	121gm	11gm	1686mg

Eggplant Manicotti

A different, delicious way to use egg-plant. Great to make ahead and freeze.

14 manicotti shells, 1 (8-oz.) box

1 medium eggplant

2 tablespoons olive oil

2 garlic cloves, minced

1/2 cup minced onion

1/2 cup water

1/2 teaspoon salt

Pepper to taste

2 cups (8 oz.) shredded low-fat mozzarella cheese

1 cup low-fat cottage cheese

1 cup fine fresh bread crumbs

2 egg whites

1/2 teaspoon dried-leaf oregano

1/2 teaspoon Italian seasoning

1 tablespoon chopped fresh parsley

4 cups spaghetti sauce

Preheat oven to 350F (175C). Cook pasta shells according to package directions; drain. Mince eggplant in a food processor fitted with the metal blade. Heat oil in a large non-stick heavy skillet over medium heat. Add garlic and sauté. Add eggplant and onion; sauté about 5 minutes. Add water, salt, pepper; cover and cook 15 minutes or until water is absorbed. In a large bowl, combine 3/4 cup mozzarella cheese, cottage cheese, bread crumbs, egg whites, oregano, Italian seasonings and parsley; mix well. Stir in eggplant mixture. Pour a small amount of spaghetti sauce in a 13" x 9" baking dish. Using a teaspoon, fill shells with eggplant mixture. Arrange shells in sauce; pour remaining sauce over shells. Sprinkle with remaining mozzarella cheese. Bake, covered, 30 minutes. Uncover; bake 15 minutes longer. Serve at once.

Yield: 7 (2-shell) servings

1 serving contains:

Cal	Prot	Fat	Chol	Carb	Fib	Sodium
463kc	21gm	18gm	20mg	57gm	1gm	1251mg

Eggplant Mozzarella

A great meal, low in all the "no-no's."

1/2 cup chopped green onion

1/2 cup sliced fresh mushrooms

1/4 cup water

2 cups spaghetti sauce

1/2 teaspoon salt

1 small eggplant, peeled, sliced

1 egg white, slightly beaten

1 tablespoon water

1/2 cup all-purpose flour

1 teaspoon olive oil

1 cup low-fat cottage cheese

1 cup (4 oz.) shredded low-fat mozzarella cheese

Variation

For an exceptionally nutritious dish, add slices of tofu between the layers.

Preheat oven to 350F (175C). In a large saucepan over low heat, cook green onion and mushrooms in 1/4 cup water until tender. Add spaghetti sauce; bring to a boil. Reduce heat; simmer 20 to 25 minutes. Sprinkle salt over sliced eggplant; set aside to drain about 10 minutes. In a shallow bowl, beat egg white and water together. Dip eggplant in egg mixture, then into flour. In a large non-stick skillet, heat a few drops of oil over medium heat. Add eggplant slices and cook until browned, turning once; drain on paper towel. Continue until all slices are cooked. In a 13" x 9" casserole, spread about 1/2 cup sauce. Add a layer of eggplant, top with 1/2 cup cottage cheese and more sauce. Repeat until all ingredients are used, ending with sauce. Sprinkle with mozzarella cheese. Bake, uncovered, 30 minutes. Let stand 5 minutes before serving.

Yield: 9 servings

1 serving contains:

Cal	Prot	Fat	Chol	Carb	Fib	Sodium
152kc	9gm	6gm	8mg	17gm	1gm	551mg

Enchilada-Bean Bake

Add nachos and salsa to complete this meal.

2 garlic cloves, minced

1/3 cup finely chopped onion

1/2 cup chopped fresh mushrooms

1/4 cup water

2 cups cooked beans, navy or pintos

1-1/2 cups stewed tomatoes

1/2 cup red wine

1 teaspoon chili powder or to taste

1 teaspoon ground cumin

1/2 cup low-fat cottage cheese

1/4 cup plain low-fat yogurt

1/4 cup shredded low-fat cheddar cheese

4 to 5 corn tortillas

Shredded lettuce, chopped green onion to garnish

Preheat oven to 350F (175C). In a large iron skillet or any large heavy skillet over low heat, cook garlic, onion and mushrooms in 1/4 cup water until tender. Add beans, tomatoes, wine, chili powder and cumin. Heat over medium-high heat until boiling; reduce heat and simmer about 30 minutes or until most of liquid is gone. Using a potato masher, mash beans thoroughly. In a small bowl, mix cottage cheese and yogurt; set aside. In a medium-size shallow casserole, put a layer of tortillas, a layer of beans and a little cheese mixture. Continue to layer until all ingredients are used, ending with cheese mixture. Sprinkle with cheddar cheese. Bake, uncovered, about 30 minutes or until bubbling. Serve immediately garnished with shredded lettuce and chopped green onion.

Yield: 6 servings

1 serving contains:

Cal	Prot	Fat	Chol	Carb	Fib	Sodium
193kc	12gm	3gm	5mg	29gm	5gm	327mg

Italian Spaghetti Squash

Low fat, low cholesterol: high flavor.

1 spaghetti squash, about 2 lbs.

4 cups hot spaghetti sauce

1/4 cup grated Parmesan cheese

Rinse squash. Cut in half lengthwise; scoop out and discard seeds. Pour water about 1 inch deep in a large, shallow saucepan. Bring to a boil and place squash, cut-side down, in boiling water. Cover and bring to a boil again. Reduce heat and simmer 40 to 50 minutes or until tender. Remove squash from pan; drain well. With a fork, scrape spaghetti-like strands from squash shell. Arrange squash strands in a large shallow serving dish. Spoon hot sauce over spaghetti squash and sprinkle with Parmesan cheese. Serve immediately.

Yield: 12 (1/2-cup) servings

1 serving contains:

Cal	Prot	Fat	Chol	Carb	Fib	Sodium
111kc	3gm	5gm	2mg	16gm	1gm	453mg

Macaroni & Cheese

New approach to an old favorite.

1 cup elbow macaroni

1 small onion, peeled, cut in half

1 sprig fresh rosemary, optional

2 cups skim milk

2 tablespoons all-purpose flour

1 tablespoon non-fat powdered milk

1/2 cup (2 oz.) shredded low-fat American cheese

1 teaspoon low-fat margarine

1/4 teaspoon salt

Pepper to taste

2 teaspoons chopped fresh parsley

Preheat oven to 350F (175C). In a large saucepan, cook macaroni in boiling water with onion and rosemary, if desired, according to directions or about 8 minutes. Drain, discarding onion and rosemary; set aside. Put 1-1/2 cups milk in a medium-size saucepan over medium heat. In a jar with a lid, combine remaining 1/2 cup milk, flour and powdered milk; shake until completely dissolved. Slowly add to warm milk in saucepan, stirring constantly, until mixture begins to thicken. Cook about 1 minute, stirring constantly. Set aside 2 tablespoons cheese. Add remaining cheese, margarine, salt and pepper to sauce; stir until cheese is melted. Pour sauce over macaroni and toss gently to coat well. Spoon into a deep 2-quart casserole. Sprinkle reserved cheese over all. Sprinkle lightly with parsley. Bake uncovered 10 minutes or until cheese melts.

Yield: 6 (1/2-cup) servings

1 serving contains:

Cal	Prot	Fat	Chol	Carb	Fib	Sodium
151kc	10gm	4gm	12mg	20gm	trace	335mg

Lasagna-Spinach Rings

Add a green salad and crusty bread for a complete dinner.

10 lasagna noodles

1 (10-oz.) pkg. thawed frozen chopped spinach

1/4 cup minced onion

2 tablespoons grated Parmesan cheese

1 cup low-fat cottage cheese

1/8 teaspoon pepper

Dash of ground nutmeg

3 cups spaghetti sauce

Preheat oven to 350F (175C). Cook noodles according to package directions; drain. Drain spinach thoroughly, then squeeze in a paper towel. In a medium-size bowl, combine spinach, onion, cheeses, pepper and nutmeg. On a clean working surface, lay a noodle out flat. Spread spinach mixture evenly along noodle, then roll up jelly-roll fashion and secure with a wooden pick. Continue until all ingredients are used. In a medium-size casserole, pour a little spaghetti sauce to cover bottom of dish; stand prepared noodles in sauce. Pour remaining sauce over noodles. Sprinkle lightly with nutmeg. Bake, uncovered, 25 to 30 minutes or until sauce is bubbling. Serve immediately.

Yield: 5 (2-noodle) servings

1 serving contains:

Cal	Prot	Fat	Chol	Carb	Fib	Sodium
359kc	16gm	9gm	4mg	56gm	2gm	1021mg

Vegetarian Lasagna

Make two, one to eat now and one to freeze.

2 carrots, shredded, about 2 cups

1 cup bite-size pieces broccoli

1 (10-oz.) thawed frozen chopped spinach, well-drained

1 cup chopped onion

1 teaspoon garlic powder

1/2 teaspoon dried leaf basil

1 teaspoon dried leaf oregano

1 tablespoon chopped fresh parsley

1/2 teaspoon seasoned salt

1 (16-oz.) box lasagna noodles

4 cups (1 lb.) shredded low-fat mozzarella cheese

2 cups low-fat cottage cheese

1/2 cup grated Parmesan cheese

2 egg whites, slightly beaten

3 cups spaghetti sauce

In a medium-size saucepan, combine carrots, broccoli, spinach, onion and all seasonings. Add just enough water to prevent mixture from sticking. Simmer 30 minutes or until all the liquid is absorbed. Meanwhile, cook lasagne noodles according to package directions. Drain and quickly rinse in cold water to stop cooking; drain again and set aside. Preheat oven to 350F (175C). Reserve 2 cups mozzarella cheese. In a small bowl, mix cottage cheese, remaining mozzarella, Parmesan and egg whites; set aside. Pour about 1/2 cup spaghetti sauce into a large lasagne pan. Place a layer of noodles over sauce; add layers of vegetables, cottage-cheese mixture and sauce. Continue layering until all ingredients are used, ending with sauce. Sprinkle remaining mozzarella over top. Bake, uncovered, 1 hour. Let stand 10 minutes before cutting.

Yield: 12 servings

1 serving contains:

Cal	Prot	Fat	Chol	Carb	Fib	Sodium
348kc	23gm	11gm	27mg	40gm	2gm	810mg

Vegetarian Pizza

What a treat—have your pizza and eat it too!

Dough:

1 (1/4-oz.) pkg. active dry yeast

1 cup warm water (110F, 45C)

1 tablespoon sugar

1 teaspoon salt

1 tablespoon plus 1 teaspoon oil of choice

1-1/2 cups whole-wheat flour

1 cup unbleached all-purpose flour

1 teaspoon cornmeal

Topping:

1-3/4 cups pizza sauce

1 medium onion, cut into rings, separated

1 green bell pepper, thinly sliced

7 to 8 fresh mushrooms, sliced

3 cups (12 oz.) shredded low-fat mozzarella cheese

2 tablespoons grated Parmesan cheese

In a mixing bowl, dissolve yeast in water. Add sugar, salt, 1 tablespoon oil, whole-wheat flour and 1/2 cup all-purpose flour; mix well. Knead in mixer with a dough hook 2 minutes on low speed. Gradually add remaining flour until dough comes away from sides of bowl. Knead on low speed about 7 minutes or until dough is smooth and elastic. Or knead by hand. With 1 teaspoon oil, grease a large bowl and two (12-inch) pizza pans. Lightly sprinkle cornmeal over pans. Put dough in greased bowl; cover and let rise in a warm place until doubled in bulk, about 1 hour. Punch down dough. Divide dough in half; press in bottom and sides of each pan. Cover and let rise in a warm place 20 minutes. Preheat oven to 425F (220C). Spread sauce over dough. Arrange onion, green pepper and mushrooms over sauce. Crumble mozzarella cheese over vegetables and sprinkle with Parmesan cheese. Bake 20 minutes or until browned and bubbling.

Yield: 6 (2-wedge) servings

1 serving contains:

Cal	Prot	Fat	Chol	Carb	Fib	Sodium
466kc	24gm	17gm	34mg	57gm	5gm	995mg

Vegetarian Stuffed Peppers

Subtle flavor blending makes these delicious! Red or yellow bell peppers can also be used.

4 green bell peppers

1/2 cup finely chopped onion

2 garlic cloves, minced

1 cup cooked long-grain white rice

1 cup finely chopped apple

2 cups creamed corn

1/3 cup fresh bread crumbs

1/4 teaspoon dill weed

1/4 teaspoon dried-leaf tarragon

1/2 teaspoon paprika

Pepper to taste

Topping:

1/2 cup fresh bread crumbs

1 teaspoon low-fat margarine, melted

1/2 cup shredded low-fat American cheese

Dash of paprika

Cut tops off peppers; remove and discard seeds. Place peppers in a large saucepan. Add water to cover and cook over medium-high heat about 5 minutes or until crisp-tender; invert over paper towel to drain well. While peppers are cooking, combine onion, garlic, rice, apple, corn, 1/3 cup bread crumbs, dill, tarragon, paprika and pepper in a medium-size bowl. Set peppers upright in a deep 8-inch-square baking dish and spoon equal amounts of stuffing into each one. Preheat oven to 350F (175C). In a small bowl, combine 1/2 cup bread crumbs, margarine and cheese. Spoon over top of each stuffed pepper; sprinkle with paprika. Bake 40 to 45 minutes. Serve immediately.

Yield: 4 servings

1 serving contains:

Cal	Prot	Fat	Chol	Carb	Fib	Sodium
375kc	11gm	5gm	8mg	76gm	3gm	686mg

Vegetable Tostadas

Serve this for a delightful, light lunch. Add Refried Beans, page 202, for a heartier meal.

1 small onion, thinly sliced

1/4 cup thinly sliced celery

1/4 cup chopped green bell pepper

1/2 cup water

2 large zucchini, thinly sliced, about 1 lb.

4 to 5 fresh mushrooms, sliced, about 1 cup

1/4 teaspoon salt

4 corn tortillas, warmed

1 cup (4 oz.) shredded low-fat cheddar cheese

1/2 cup plain low-fat yogurt

2 tomatoes, chopped, about 1-1/4 cups

1/4 cup salsa

In a large non-stick skillet over medium-high heat, cook onion, celery and green pepper in 1/2 cup water 3 to 4 minutes or until tender. Add zucchini, mushrooms and salt; cook about 4 minutes longer or until vegetables are crisp-tender; drain well. Lay warm tortillas on a baking sheet; divide vegetable mixture evenly over tortillas. Sprinkle with shredded cheese. Place in a 350F (175C) oven 3 to 5 minutes or until cheese melts. Top with yogurt, tomatoes and salsa. Serve immediately.

Yield: 2 (2-tostada) servings

1 serving contains:

Cal	Prot	Fat	Chol	Carb	Fib	Sodium
419kc	28gm	15gm	44mg	50gm	8gm	952mg

Vegetables & Rice

Vegetables play a very important role in our meals. They provide vitamins, minerals and fiber, while at the same time adding color and flavor.

Always choose the freshest possible vegetables. Use them as close as possible to the time of purchase. This may mean shopping for produce twice a week, but the nutritional results are worth the extra trip to the store. Always wash vegetables well just prior to cooking. Cook with skins on if possible; precious vitamins are lost with the peelings. Use a small amount of water so the water-soluble vitamins are retained. The most important point to remember about cooking vegetables is not to overcook. Cook just until barely tender.

Herbs and spices add zest to all vegetables. Take advantage of the wide variety of herbs available today. I eliminate salt by using herbs. Use herbs sparingly at first, then experiment with increased amounts. See the herb section, page 17.

I like to liven up steamed grean beans with a touch of low-fat margarine and a sprinkling of dill weed or tarragon. Fresh chopped or dried-leaf basil works well with crisp-tender carrots. A small amount of low-fat shredded cheese also gives a tasty final touch to simply cooked vegetables. My family enjoys broccoli dusted with grated Parmesan cheese. Halved tomatoes broiled with a little cheese and basil on top make an appealing side dish with poached fish. Next time you plan an outdoor get-together, put some of your favorite vegetables such as zucchini, yellow squash, cherry tomatoes, mushrooms or onion wedges on skewers. They can be brushed with a little oil from time to time or basted with your favorite barbecue sauce.

We enjoy the nutty flavor of brown rice, and hope you'll try it too. Brown-Rice Pilaf is a great basic dish. You can personalize it by adding your favorite spices and vegetables.

Hopping John is a traditional Southern dish, combining rice and black-eyed peas.

Ann's Green Beans with Orange Sauce

The sweet-sour orange sauce makes this special.

1 (9-oz.) pkg. frozen French-cut green beans

2 tablespoons sugar

1/2 tablespoon cornstarch

1/8 teaspoon salt

1/8 teaspoon ground allspice

1 teaspoon vinegar

2 tablespoons water

1/2 tablespoon finely grated orange peel

1 teaspoon low-fat margarine

Place frozen green beans in a 1-quart casserole with 2 tablespoons water; cover. Microwave 4 minutes on HIGH; stir then cook 4 minutes longer. Or cook beans according to package directions. Drain cooked beans. While beans are cooking, combine sugar, cornstarch, salt and allspice in a small saucepan. Stir in vinegar and water. Stir over medium-high heat until sauce begins to boil and thicken; cook 1 minute longer. Remove from heat. Add orange peel and margarine; stir until well blended. Place beans in a serving dish. Pour sauce over beans and toss gently. Serve immediately.

Yield: 4 (scant 1/2-cup) servings

1 serving contains:

Cal	Prot	Fat	Chol	Carb	Fib	Sodium
44kc	1gm	1gm	0	10gm	1gm	81mg

Green Beans & Dill

Dill makes it different!

**2 cups prepared fresh or frozen
green beans**

**2 tablespoons sliced fresh
mushrooms**

2 tablespoons chopped pimiento

1 teaspoon low-fat margarine

1/2 teaspoon dill weed

Strips of lemon peel, optional

Put about 1/2 cup water into a medium-size saucepan. Add beans and cook over medium-low heat until nearly tender. Add mushrooms and cook 1 minute longer. Drain and add pimiento, margarine and dill; toss gently to mix. Remove from heat. Cover and let stand a few minutes before serving. To serve, garnish with lemon peel, if desired.

Yield: 4 (1/2-cup) servings

1 serving contains:

Cal	Prot	Fat	Chol	Carb	Fib	Sodium
29kc	1gm	1gm	0	6gm	1gm	14mg

Spanish Lima Beans

A colorful combination dish.

1 cup frozen lima beans

1/2 cup water

1 tablespoon chopped onion

1/2 bay leaf

1/2 cup fresh or frozen whole-kernel corn

1/2 cup chopped fresh or canned tomatoes

1/4 teaspoon dried-leaf marjoram

1 teaspoon low-fat margarine

1/4 teaspoon salt

Pepper to taste

Put beans, water, onion and bay leaf into a medium-size saucepan; cook about 10 minutes over medium heat. Add corn, tomatoes, marjoram, margarine, salt and pepper; cook about 15 minutes longer or until lima beans are tender. Drain and serve immediately.

Yield: 3 (1/2-cup) servings

1 serving contains:

Cal	Prot	Fat	Chol	Carb	Fib	Sodium
94kc	5gm	1gm	0	18gm	4gm	275mg

Candied Acorn Squash

Use "lite" maple syrup because it has half the calories of regular syrup.

2 acorn squash

4 tablespoons "lite" maple syrup

2 teaspoons low-fat margarine

1/8 teaspoon ground allspice

Preheat oven to 375F (190C). Wash squash and cut in half; remove seeds and stringy parts. Place squash halves, cut side up, in a medium-size shallow baking dish. Put 1 tablespoon syrup and 1/2 teaspoon margarine in each half; dust with allspice. Bake, covered, 35 minutes, then uncover and bake about 15 minutes longer or until tender. Serve immediately.

Yield: 4 servings

1 serving contains:

Cal	Prot	Fat	Chol	Carb	Fib	Sodium
125kc	2gm	1gm	0	30gm	3gm	30mg

Scalloped Turnips

You'll be proud to take this casserole anywhere.

1 lb. turnips, about 3 small

1/2 cup skim milk

1 teaspoon low-fat margarine

1/4 cup shredded low-fat American cheese

1/2 cup fresh bread crumbs

Dash of ground ginger

1/8 teaspoon salt

Dash of pepper

1 tablespoon grated Parmesan cheese

Peel and slice turnips. Put in a medium-size saucepan and add water to cover. Bring to a boil, then reduce heat. Cover and simmer 12 to 15 minutes or just until tender; drain well. Preheat oven to 350F (175C). While turnips are cooking, heat milk and margarine in a small saucepan. When hot but not boiling quickly stir in American cheese until melted. Add crumbs, ginger, salt and pepper. Pour over turnips, tossing gently to coat well. Spoon into a 1-quart casserole and sprinkle with Parmesan cheese. Bake 15 minutes, then put under preheated broiler until top is browned. Serve immediately.

Yield: 4 (1/2-cup) servings

1 serving contains:

Cal	Prot	Fat	Chol	Carb	Fib	Sodium
107kc	6gm	3gm	6mg	16gm	1gm	336mg

Brown-Rice Pilaf

Brown rice retains the original nutrients of the rice kernel. The nutty flavor complements chicken or seafood dishes.

2 tablespoons chopped onion

1 cup plus 2 tablespoons water

1 cup brown rice

2 cups chicken broth

1/4 teaspoon rubbed sage

Variations

Sherried Brown-Rice Pilaf: Omit sage. Cook 1/2 cup sliced fresh mushrooms with onion. Combine with rice and bake as directed. When done, stir in 3 tablespoons sherry.

Preheat oven to 350F (175C). In a medium-size saucepan over medium heat, cook onion in 2 tablespoons water until tender. Add rice and stir constantly until heated. Stir in chicken broth, 1 cup water and sage; bring to a boil. Pour into a 2-quart ovenproof casserole. Bake, covered, 50 to 60 minutes or until liquid is absorbed and rice is tender. Fluff with a fork before serving.

Yield: 6 (1/2-cup) servings

1 serving contains:

Cal	Prot	Fat	Chol	Carb	Fib	Sodium
130kc	4gm	1gm	trace	25gm	3gm	259mg

Hopping John

This Southern favorite brings good luck when eaten on New Year's Day. Top with spicy salsa.

1/2 cup chopped green bell pepper

1/2 cup chopped onion

1/4 cup water

6 cups cooked black-eyed peas

2 cups cooked long-grain rice

**1/4 teaspoon red (cayenne) pepper
  or to taste**

In a large saucepan over low heat, cook green pepper and onion in water until tender. Stir in beans, rice and red pepper. Cook over low heat until most of liquid is absorbed. Serve immediately.

Yield: 16 (1/2-cup) servings

1 serving contains:

Cal	Prot	Fat	Chol	Carb	Fib	Sodium
98kc	6gm	1gm	0	18gm	trace	4mg

Slow-baked Beans

Great for a picnic.

3 cups cooked pinto beans

3 cups cooked lima beans

1/4 cup catsup

3 tablespoons firmly packed brown sugar

1/2 cup chopped onion

2 large fresh tomatoes, cut into eighths, about 2-1/2 cups

1 cup chopped green bell pepper

Preheat oven to 350F (175C). Combine beans, catsup, brown sugar, onion, tomatoes and green pepper in a 3-quart casserole. Bake, covered, 2-1/2 hours. If beans have too much liquid, remove lid for final 30 minutes; stir occasionally. Serve hot or warm.

Yield: 10 (1/2-cup) servings

1 serving contains:

Cal	Prot	Fat	Chol	Carb	Fib	Sodium
121kc	5gm	trace	0	25gm	4gm	75mg

Refried Beans

Perfect side dish with Chicken Fajitas, page 149. Sprinkle with 1/2 cup shredded low-fat cheddar cheese for extra flavor.

1/4 cup chopped onion

1 garlic clove, minced

1/4 cup chicken broth

1 cup cooked tomatoes, seeds removed

1/4 cup diced green chilies

1/2 cup white wine

1/4 tablespoon chili powder

1 teaspoon ground cumin

6 cups cooked pinto beans

In a large soup kettle over low heat, cook onion and garlic in broth. Add tomatoes, chilies, wine, chili powder, cumin and beans; bring to a boil. Reduce heat to medium low and simmer about 45 minutes. Heat a large, deep iron skillet or any large heavy skillet over medium low. With a slotted spoon, lift some beans out of liquid and put into skillet. Mash with a potato masher, keeping beans in constant motion. Continue adding and mashing remaining beans. Serve immediately.

Yield: 10 (1/2-cup) servings

1 serving contains:

Cal	Prot	Fat	Chol	Carb	Fib	Sodium
73kc	4gm	trace	trace	13gm	2gm	60mg

Red Cabbage

Good make-ahead side dish that's even more delicious the second day.

1 teaspoon oil of choice

1/2 cup finely chopped onion

4 cups coarsely shredded red cabbage, about 1/2 head

1 cup chopped peeled apple

2 whole cloves

1/2 bay leaf

1 tablespoon sugar

1-1/2 tablespoons white vinegar

In a heavy skillet, heat oil over medium-high heat. Add onion and sauté until tender. Add cabbage, apple, cloves and bay leaf. Cover and simmer about 20 minutes or until cabbage is tender. If cabbage gets dry, add a small amount of water. Add sugar and vinegar to cabbage mixture; toss gently. Cover and cook about 5 minutes longer. Serve immediately.

Yield: 6 (3/4-cup) servings

1 serving contains:

Cal	Prot	Fat	Chol	Carb	Fib	Sodium
45kc	1gm	1gm	0	9gm	2gm	5mg

Gingered Carrots

Colorful for a special dinner.

6 medium-size carrots, peeled, cut into 1-inch pieces

1 tablespoon sugar

1 teaspoon cornstarch

1/8 teaspoon ground nutmeg

1/4 teaspoon ground ginger

1/4 cup orange juice

1 teaspoon low-fat margarine

Steam carrots just until tender; drain. While carrots are cooking, combine sugar, cornstarch, nutmeg and ginger in a small saucepan; add orange juice. Cook over medium heat, stirring constantly, until sauce thickens. Cook 1 minute, then remove from heat and stir in margarine. Place carrots in a serving dish; pour sauce over them, tossing to coat evenly. Cover and let stand 4 to 5 minutes before serving.

Yield: 6 (1/2-cup) servings

1 serving contains:

Cal	Prot	Fat	Chol	Carb	Fib	Sodium
52kc	1gm	1gm	0	12gm	3gm	60mg

Carrots & Squash

Add color with summer squash and pattypan squash.

3 medium-size carrots, peeled

1 zucchini

1/2 cup chicken broth

1/4 teaspoon Mrs. Dash® herb seasoning

Slice carrots and zucchini lengthwise into fourths, then cut into about 2-inch lengths. In a medium-size saucepan over medium heat, cook vegetables in chicken broth until just tender. Drain, then return vegetables to warm pan. Add seasoning and toss gently. Cover and let stand a few minutes before serving.

Yield: 5 (1/2-cup) servings

1 serving contains:

Cal	Prot	Fat	Chol	Carb	Fib	Sodium
29kc	1gm	trace	trace	6gm	2gm	109mg

Glazed Carrots & Zucchini

Tasty and colorful.

4 medium-size carrots, peeled, cut into pieces

1 zucchini, cut into pieces

1 teaspoon low-fat margarine

1 teaspoon sugar

1 teaspoon lemon juice

Steam carrots about 10 minutes. Add zucchini and steam just until tender. Drain water from pan and return vegetables to warm pan. Add margarine, sugar and lemon juice; toss gently to coat. Cover and let stand 3 to 4 minutes before serving.

Yield: 6 (1/2-cup) servings

1 serving contains:

Cal	Prot	Fat	Chol	Carb	Fib	Sodium
32kc	1gm	trace	0	7gm	2gm	43mg

Zippy Cauliflower

Green chilies and cheese pack it with flavor.

3 cups cauliflower, flowerets and some stems

1/2 teaspoon low-fat margarine

1 tablespoon all-purpose flour

1/8 teaspoon red (cayenne) pepper

1/4 teaspoon salt

1/8 teaspoon pepper

3/4 cup skim milk

1/2 cup shredded low-fat cheddar cheese

2 tablespoons chopped green chilies

1/4 cup fresh bread crumbs

Preheat oven to 350F (175C). Steam cauliflower just until tender; drain. Melt margarine in a medium-size saucepan over medium heat. In a jar with a lid, combine flour, red pepper, salt, pepper and milk; shake until blended. Slowly add to margarine in saucepan, stirring constantly until smooth. Add cheese and continue stirring until smooth and slightly thickened. Stir in chilies. Arrange cauliflower in a 2-quart baking dish; pour sauce over cauliflower, then sprinkle with bread crumbs. Bake 10 to 15 minutes or until bubbling. Serve immediately.

Yield: 6 (1/2-cup) servings

1 serving contains:

Cal	Prot	Fat	Chol	Carb	Fib	Sodium
73kc	5gm	2gm	7mg	9gm	1gm	209mg

Shredded Sweet Potatoes

Your food processor makes it quick and easy.

**2 medium sweet potatoes, shred-
ded, about 4 cups**

1 teaspoon oil of choice

1/2 cup chopped onion

1/2 teaspoon Butter Buds®

1/8 teaspoon ground ginger

Variation

Sweet-Potato Pancake: Increase oil to 1
tablespoon and sauté onion as above.
Add shredded potatoes combined
with Butter Buds and ginger, pressing
and cooking like a large pancake.
When brown and crisp, turn pancake
over and cook other side until done.

Thoroughly scrub potatoes; cut off tips
and peel. Shred potatoes and set aside.
Heat oil in a non-stick skillet over medium heat. Add onion; sauté until tender. Add sweet potatoes, Butter Buds,
and ginger. Cook over medium heat, stirring occasionaly until potatoes are tender. Serve immediately.

Yield: 6 (1/2-cup) servings

1 serving contains:

Cal	Prot	Fat	Chol	Carb	Fib	Sodium
51kc	1gm	1gm	0	10gm	1gm	6mg

Potato Cakes

Always a favorite with children.

2 cups mashed potatoes

1 egg white, slightly beaten

2 tablespoons chopped onion

2 tablespoons all-purpose flour

1/8 teaspoon salt

Pepper to taste

1 teaspoon oil of choice

In a medium-size bowl, combine potatoes, egg white, onion, flour, salt and pepper. Meanwhile, heat oil in a large skillet over medium-high heat. When hot, put about 2 tablespoons potato mixture for each cake into skillet. Cook until well-browned, then turn with a spatula and cook other side until brown. Continue making cakes with remaining mixture, keeping first ones warm. Serve immediately.

Yield: 6 (3-inch-cake) servings

1 serving contains:

Cal	Prot	Fat	Chol	Carb	Fib	Sodium
74kc	2gm	1gm	1mg	15gm	trace	260mg

Potato-Cheese Puff

Potato casserole with a unique flavor.

2 cups mashed potatoes

1 tablespoon minced onion

2 tablespoons skim milk

1 cup low-fat cottage cheese

1/2 teaspoon Butter Buds®

Paprika to taste

Preheat oven to 350F (175C). In a medium-size bowl, combine potatoes, onion, milk, cottage cheese and Butter Buds. Spoon into a 1-quart casserole; sprinkle with paprika. Bake, uncovered, 25 minutes or until beginning to brown. Serve immediately.

Yield: 5 (1/2-cup) servings

1 serving contains:

Cal	Prot	Fat	Chol	Carb	Fib	Sodium
107kc	7gm	1gm	2mg	18gm	1gm	193mg

Scalloped Potatoes

Serve this reduced-calorie traditional dish with Turkey Loaf, page 155.

About 2 lbs. potatoes, peeled, sliced

1/3 cup chopped onion

3 tablespoons all-purpose flour

1/2 teaspoon salt

1/4 teaspoon pepper

1 tablespoon low-fat margarine

3 cups skim milk, heated

Preheat oven to 400F (205C). Lightly spray a 2-quart casserole with vegetable spray. Arrange a layer of potatoes in casserole, then sprinkle with some of onion, flour, salt and pepper. Continue to layer until all potatoes, onion, flour, salt and pepper are used. Dot top with margarine, then pour milk over all. Bake 20 minutes, then reduce heat to 350F (175C) and bake 50 to 60 minutes longer or until tender. Serve immediately.

Yield: 6 (3/4-cup) servings

1 serving contains:

Cal	Prot	Fat	Chol	Carb	Fib	Sodium
166kc	7gm	1gm	2mg	32gm	2gm	225mg

Pennsylvania Sweet Potatoes in Tangy Sauce

Different sweet potatoes for your holiday menu.

6 large sweet potatoes, scrubbed

1 cup granulated sugar

1/2 cup lightly packed brown sugar

1/4 teaspoon ground ginger

2 tablespoons cornstarch

1 cup unsweetened pineapple juice

1 teaspoon lemon juice

1 tablespoon low-fat margarine

Place sweet potatoes in a large kettle and add water to cover. Cook over medium heat until barely tender; drain. Peel and cut potatoes into fourths. Arrange in a medium-size casserole. Preheat oven to 350F (175C). While potatoes are cooking, combine sugars, ginger and cornstarch in a small saucepan. Add pineapple juice and lemon juice. Stir over medium heat until sugars are dissolved and mixture starts to bubble; stir in margarine. Pour sauce over potatoes. Bake, uncovered, 50 to 60 minutes or until sauce is thickened. Serve immediately.

Yield: Approximately 10 (1/2-cup) servings

1 serving contains:

Cal	Prot	Fat	Chol	Carb	Fib	Sodium
149kc	1gm	trace	0	37gm	1gm	18mg

Oven French Fries

So much better than the old greasy kind.

6 medium potatoes, washed, about 3 lbs.

2 tablespoons oil of choice

1 (1-oz.) pkg. Good Seasons® Italian Dressing, not mixed

1 tablespoon chopped fresh parsley

Preheat oven to 350F (175C). Peel potatoes and slice for French fries. Lay them out on several layers of paper towel to absorb moisture; pat dry with another paper towel. Potatoes should be as dry as possible. Put potatoes in a large bowl and drizzle with oil, tossing to coat evenly. Lay in a single layer on a large baking sheet; sprinkle dry dressing mix and parsley over all. Bake 25 minutes, then flip them over with a turner; only do this once. Return to oven and increase temperature to 450F (175C). Cook 3 to 5 minutes longer or until potatoes are tender and start to brown. Serve immediately.

Yield: 4 servings

1 serving contains:

Cal	Prot	Fat	Chol	Carb	Fib	Sodium
239kc	4gm	7gm	0	42gm	2gm	256mg

Brown Rice

Keep small portions in your freezer to add to other dishes.

2 tablespoons grated onion

3 cups plus 2 tablespoons water

1 cup uncooked long-grain brown rice

In a medium-size saucepan over low heat, cook onion in 2 tablespoons water until tender. Add rice, stirring until heated. Add remaining water; cover and bring to a boil. Reduce heat to low and simmer about 1 hour or until all liquid is absorbed and rice is tender. Fluff with a fork before serving.

Yield: 6 (1/2-cup) servings

1 serving contains:

Cal	Prot	Fat	Chol	Carb	Fib	Sodium
117kc	2gm	1gm	0	25gm	3gm	trace

Rice & Green Onion

A green-rice casserole.

3/4 cup thinly sliced green onion

1/2 cup chopped green bell pepper

1 teaspoon oil of choice

1 cup uncooked long-grain white rice

1/4 cup chopped fresh parsley

2 cups hot chicken broth

Pepper to taste

Preheat oven to 350F (175C). In a medium-size saucepan, sauté green onion and green pepper in oil over medium heat. Add rice, parsley, broth and pepper; bring to a boil. Pour into a 2-quart casserole. Bake, covered, 20 minutes or until all liquid is absorbed and rice is tender. Fluff with a fork before serving.

Yield: 6 (1/2-cup) servings

1 serving contains:

Cal	Prot	Fat	Chol	Carb	Fib	Sodium
139kc	4gm	1gm	0	27gm	1gm	265mg

Rice & Pecan Pilaf

Pecans are optional, depending on your diet limitations.

1 teaspoon low-fat margarine

1/2 cup chopped pecans

1/4 cup chopped onion

1 cup uncooked long-grain white rice

2 cups hot chicken broth

1/8 teaspoon dried-leaf thyme

1/8 teaspoon pepper

1 tablespoon chopped fresh parsley

Preheat oven to 350F (175C). Melt 1/2 teaspoon margarine in a medium-size skillet over medium-high heat. Add pecans and sauté about 2 minutes. Remove from skillet and set aside. Melt remaining 1/2 teaspoon margarine in skillet; add onion and sauté until tender. Add rice and stir to coat. Add chicken broth, thyme, pepper and parsley. Cover and bring to a boil. Pour into a 2-quart casserole. Bake, covered, 17 minutes or until all liquid is absorbed and rice is tender. Just before serving, stir in nuts and fluff.

Yield: 6 (1/2-cup) servings

1 serving contains:

Cal	Prot	Fat	Chol	Carb	Fib	Sodium
190kc	4gm	7gm	trace	27gm	1gm	268mg

Variation

Stove-Top Rice & Pecan Pilaf: Cook on top of the stove in the skillet by simmering, covered, 18 to 20 minutes.

Lou's Grilled Vegetables

Make ahead for your cookout.

4 potatoes, scrubbed, thinly sliced, about 3 cups

4 carrots, thinly sliced, slightly cooked, about 3 cups

2 onions, cut into rings, about 2 cups

2 zucchini, medium sliced, about 2 cups

24 cherry tomatoes, cut in half

1-1/2 teaspoons low-fat margarine

1/4 teaspoon salt

Pepper to taste

Heat grill. Divide potatoes, carrots, onions and zucchini among 6 large pieces of heavy-duty aluminum foil. Put 4 cherry tomatoes, then 1/4 teaspoon margarine on each stack. Add salt and pepper. Fold foil over several times to seal tightly. Vegetables can be made a few hours ahead to this point and refrigerated. Place foil packages on a medium-hot grill about 30 minutes, turning occasionally, until vegetables are tender. Serve immediately.

Yield: 6 servings

1 serving contains:

Cal	Prot	Fat	Chol	Carb	Fib	Sodium
162kc	4gm	1gm	0	36gm	7gm	123mg

Mexican Vegetable Casserole

Cilantro complements this dish nicely.

1 teaspoon olive oil

1 large onion, cut into 6 wedges

1 large green bell pepper, cut into 1/2-inch pieces

1 small eggplant, cut into wedges (do not peel)

1-1/2 tablespoons all-purpose flour

2 medium-size tomatoes, cut in wedges

1 zucchini, sliced

1/3 cup diced canned green chilies

1/2 teaspoon dried-leaf basil

1/8 teaspoon pepper

1/2 teaspoon salt

Dash of red-pepper sauce or to taste

Preheat oven to 350F (175C). Heat oil in a large non-stick skillet over medium-high heat. Add onion and green pepper; sauté until tender. Coat eggplant with flour. Add to skillet and stir gently but quickly until coated with oil. Add tomatoes, zucchini, chilies, basil, pepper, salt and red-pepper sauce. Spoon into a medium-size casserole. Bake, covered, 25 to 30 minutes or until vegetables are just tender. Serve immediately.

Yield: 9 (3/4-cup) servings

1 serving contains:

Cal	Prot	Fat	Chol	Carb	Fib	Sodium
33 kc	1gm	1gm	0	6gm	2gm	113mg

Stir-fried Vegetables

Enhances any meal.

1 tablespoon oil of choice

1 garlic clove, minced

1 thin slice fresh ginger root, minced

4 cups prepared fresh raw vegetables*

2 to 3 tablespoons water

2 tablespoons soy sauce

1 tablespoon cornstarch

1/2 cup chicken broth

Heat wok or a large non-stick skillet; add oil and heat over medium high. Stir-fry garlic and ginger about 5 seconds. Add vegetables and stir-fry quickly about 1 minute to coat with oil. Stir-fry about 2 minutes longer. Add water to pan; cover and steam 2 to 3 minutes. Stir in soy sauce. In a small bowl, blend cornstarch and broth. Pour over vegetables and cook about 30 seconds longer or until sauce thickens. Serve immediately.

Yield: 7 (1/2-cup) servings

1 serving contains:

Cal	Prot	Fat	Chol	Carb	Fib	Sodium
45kc	2gm	2gm	trace	5gm	1gm	364mg

Suggested vegetables:

Asparagus, cut into 2-inch pieces
Bell peppers, cut into chunks
Broccoli, cut into flowerets, stems
   sliced
Cabbage, coarsely sliced
Carrots, thinly sliced
Cauliflower, cut into flowerets
Celery, thinly sliced diagonally
Green beans, cut into 2-inch pieces
Mushrooms, thickly sliced
Onion, sliced
Snow peas, whole
Water chestnuts, medium sliced
Zucchini, medium sliced

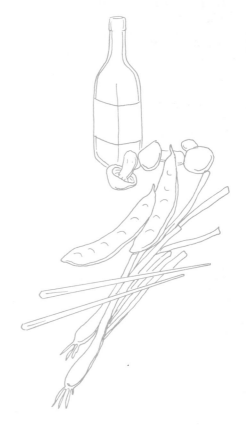

Tomato Slices with Herbs

A wonderful summer treat.

3 medium-size tomatoes, about 1 lb.

2/3 cup fresh bread crumbs

1 tablespoon low-fat margarine, melted

1/4 teaspoon dried-leaf basil

Preheat oven to 350F (175C). Slice tomatoes and arrange in a medium-size shallow baking dish. Put crumbs in a small bowl and stir in margarine and basil. Sprinkle crumb mixture over tomatoes. Bake, uncovered, 5 to 6 minutes or until crumbs are brown. Serve immediately.

Yield: 6 servings

1 serving contains:

Cal	Prot	Fat	Chol	Carb	Fib	Sodium
65kc	2gm	2gm	0	11gm	1gm	109mg

Zucchini & Mushrooms

Great flavor and quick and easy to make.

3 medium-size zucchini, about 1-1/4 lbs.

1/2 teaspoon low-fat margarine

5 or 6 fresh mushrooms, sliced, about 4 oz.

1 teaspoon dried-leaf basil

Pepper to taste

Butter-Buds® to taste

Rinse zucchini; cut into fourths lengthwise, then cut into pieces. Steam zucchini until crisp-tender. While zucchini is cooking, melt margarine in a small non-stick skillet over medium-high heat. Add mushrooms and sauté quickly. Drain zucchini and return with mushrooms to dry steamer saucepan without steamer. Add basil, pepper and Butter Buds; toss gently. Cover and let stand a few minutes before serving.

Yield: 6 (1/2-cup) servings

1 serving contains:

Cal	Prot	Fat	Chol	Carb	Fib	Sodium
21kc	2gm	trace	0	4gm	2gm	11mg

Stuffed Zucchini

A pretty dish that goes together quickly.

2 medium-size zucchini, about 1 lb.

About 1/4 cup chicken broth

3 tablespoons finely chopped fresh mushrooms

1 tablespoon finely chopped onion

1 tablespoon finely chopped green bell pepper

1/2 teaspoon dried-leaf basil

1/4 teaspoon dried-leaf oregano

2 tablespoons fresh bread crumbs

1 cup tomato sauce

1 tablespoon shredded low-fat cheddar cheese

Preheat oven to 350F (175C). Rinse zucchini; cut lengthwise into halves. Scoop out centers and chop pulp fine. Put chicken broth into a medium-size non-stick skillet over medium-high heat. Add pulp, mushrooms, onion, green pepper, basil and oregano; cook until limp. Remove from heat. Add bread crumbs and toss well. Add more broth if needed to make stuffing stick together. Fill zucchini shells with stuffing. Pour a little tomato sauce into a shallow medium-size baking dish. Place stuffed zucchini in dish and pour remaining tomato sauce over all. Bake, uncovered, 25 to 30 minutes; sprinkle with cheese and bake 5 minutes longer. Serve immediately.

Yield: 4 servings

1 serving contains:

Cal	Prot	Fat	Chol	Carb	Fib	Sodium
62kc	4gm	1gm	1mg	11gm	2gm	106mg

Zucchini & Tomato Casserole

A wonderful summer dish.

4 zucchini, cut into cubes, about 1-1/4 lbs.

Pepper to taste

1 tablespoon snipped chives

1 teaspoon low-fat margarine, melted

2 large tomatoes, sliced

1 teaspoon dried-leaf basil

1/2 cup shredded low-fat cheddar cheese

Preheat oven to 350F (175C). Steam zucchini until crisp-tender. Using a slotted spoon, transfer zucchini to a shallow 2-quart casserole. Stir pepper and chives into margarine and pour over zucchini. Cover with tomato slices; sprinkle with basil and cheese. Bake, uncovered, 30 minutes. Serve immediately.

Yield: 6 servings

1 serving contains:

Cal	Prot	Fat	Chol	Carb	Fib	Sodium
54kc	4gm	2gm	7mg	5gm	2gm	84mg

Southwest Zucchini Casserole

Zucchini, chilies and cheese are a real Tucson treat.

4 small zucchini, about 1-1/4 lbs.

1/2 cup minced onion

1/2 cup minced celery

1/4 cup water

1/4 cup diced canned green chilies

Salt and pepper to taste

1/2 cup shredded low-fat cheddar cheese

Rinse zucchini; cut in fourths lengthwise, then cut into pieces. In a small saucepan over low heat, cook onion and celery in water until tender; set aside. Steam zucchini until crisp-tender. Preheat broiler. Put zucchini in a 2-quart casserole and add onion, celery, green chilies, salt and pepper; toss gently to combine. Sprinkle cheese over top and place under broiler just until melted and cheese is starting to brown. Serve immediately.

Yield: 5 (1/2-cup) servings

1 serving contains:

Cal	Prot	Fat	Chol	Carb	Fib	Sodium
57kc	5gm	2gm	8mg	6gm	2gm	97mg

Sauces & Gravies

Sauces and gravies add a totally new dimension to the most mundane foods. Here is a wide variety of sauces to complement many dishes—from Cheese Sauce for vegetables or entrees to Chocolate Sauce for an otherwise plain low-fat white cake. Rediscover the joy of a garnished baked potato when guilt-free Sour-Cream Substitute becomes a staple in your refrigerator. Use it plain, or add chopped chives. For an even more exciting taste, add dried dill weed to the "mock" sour cream and let it stand about 2 hours so the flavors can blend.

Always use low-fat ingredients and stir well. For a cooked sauce or gravy, use a heavy saucepan to help prevent sticking.

Some recipes can be frozen, such as Grandma's Barbecue Sauce, Marinara Sauce and Tomato Sauce. Other sauces like Herb Margarine, Chocolate Sauce and Sour-Cream Substitute will keep in the refrigerator several days and can be used as needed.

While these sauces are much lower in fat, cholesterol and calories than traditional recipes, they must still be used with discretion. Always take into consideration your total fat, cholesterol and calories for the day. Plan your menu accordingly.

Chicken Milk Gravy

No need to add salt if you use canned broth or seasoned homemade broth.

2-1/2 tablespoons cornstarch

1/4 cup non-fat powdered milk

2 cups chicken broth

Pepper to taste

In a medium-size saucepan, thoroughly blend cornstarch and powdered milk; gradually stir in broth. Cook over medium-high heat, stirring constantly, until mixture thickens. Add pepper to taste.

Yield: 2 cups or 8 (1/4-cup) servings

1 serving contains:

Cal	Prot	Fat	Chol	Carb	Fib	Sodium
26kc	2gm	trace	1mg	4gm	0	206mg

Chicken Gravy

Use your own unsalted homemade broth and the sodium content is much lower than given below.

2 cups chicken broth

2-1/2 tablespoons cornstarch

Pepper to taste

In a cup, thoroughly blend a small amount of broth and cornstarch. Add to remaining broth in a medium-size saucepan. Cook over medium-high heat, stirring constantly, until gravy thickens. Add pepper to taste.

Yield: 2 cups or 8 (1/4-cup) servings

1 serving contains:

Cal	Prot	Fat	Chol	Carb	Fib	Sodium
19kc	1gm	trace	trace	2gm	0	194mg

Cheese Sauce

A real treat to serve over steamed vegetables.

1 tablespoon low-fat margarine

1/4 teaspoon salt

1/8 teaspoon pepper

1/4 teaspoon dry mustard

3/4 cup skim milk

1 tablespoon all-purpose flour

1/2 cup shredded low-fat American or cheddar cheese

In a small heavy saucepan, melt margarine over medium heat; add salt, pepper and dry mustard. In a small jar with a lid, combine milk and flour; shake well until blended. Slowly stir milk mixture into margarine in saucepan. Add cheese and cook over medium heat, stirring constantly, until sauce has thickened slightly.

Yield: 1-1/4 cups or 10 (2-tablespoon) servings

1 serving contains:

Cal	Prot	Fat	Chol	Carb	Fib	Sodium
30kc	2gm	2gm	4mg	2gm	trace	114mg

Cucumber Sauce for Fish

Clean fresh flavor for your favorite fish.

1 medium cucumber, peeled, shredded

1 cup Sour-Cream Substitute, page 241

2 tablespoons low-fat mayonnaise-type salad dressing

1 teaspoon dill weed

1 teaspoon lemon juice

Pepper to taste

In a small bowl, combine cucumber, Sour-Cream Substitute, salad dressing, dill weed, lemon juice and pepper. Cover and refrigerate 1 to 2 hours, then bring close to room temperature shortly before serving. When fish is ready to serve, gently place on a serving platter and spoon sauce over fish.

Yield: 1-1/2 cups or 12 (2-tablespoon) servings

1 serving contains:

Cal	Prot	Fat	Chol	Carb	Fib	Sodium
26kc	3gm	1gm	2mg	2gm	trace	79mg

Caper Sauce

Creamy caper sauce perks up your fish recipes.

1/2 cup Sour-Cream Substitute, page 241

2 tablespoons drained capers

1/4 teaspoon brown mustard

1/2 teaspoon lemon juice

In a small bowl, blend Sour-Cream Substitute, capers, mustard and lemon juice. Cover and refrigerate 1 to 2 hours, then bring close to room temperature shortly before serving. When fish is ready to serve, gently place on a serving platter and spoon sauce over fish.

Yield: 3/4 cup or 6 (2-tablespoon) servings

1 serving contains:

Cal	Prot	Fat	Chol	Carb	Fib	Sodium
16kc	2gm	trace	1mg	1gm	trace	81mg

Tomato Sauce

When tomatoes are in season, freeze to use later as a base for sauces such as Marinara Sauce, page 237.

2 lbs. fresh tomatoes

2 tablespoons finely chopped onion

1 garlic clove

1 tablespoon minced fresh parsley

1 teaspoon dried-leaf basil or dill weed

Mark tomatoes with a small *X* at the non-blossom end, then put in boiling water for 1 minute. Plunge tomatoes into iced water for 1 minute, then peel. Cut into quarters and put in a medium-size saucepan with onion and garlic. Bring to a boil; reduce heat to low and simmer, uncovered, until vegetables are tender. Put vegetables through a food mill, or purée in a blender or food processor fitted with the metal blade; strain to remove seeds. Return puréed mixture to saucepan with herbs. Cook over low heat 1 to 2 hours or until thickened. Use in chicken or pasta dishes, or serve warm with poached fish.

Yield: About 3-1/2 cups or 7 (1/2-cup) servings

1 serving contains:

Cal	Prot	Fat	Chol	Carb	Fib	Sodium
28kc	1gm	trace	0	6gm	2gm	11mg

Grandma's Barbecue Sauce

Always a favorite basting sauce for family get-togethers.

2 cups stewed tomatoes

1/2 cup water

1/2 cup tomato catsup

1/2 cup Worcestershire sauce

1 cup finely chopped onion

1 garlic clove, minced

1/2 cup vinegar

1 tablespoon sugar

1/8 teaspoon red (cayenne) pepper

1/8 teaspoon black pepper

1/4 teaspoon dry mustard

2 teaspoons low-fat margarine

Put tomatoes through a food mill or process in a food processor fitted with the metal blade; strain out seeds. Put strained tomatoes, water, catsup, Worcestershire sauce, onion, garlic, vinegar and sugar into a medium-size saucepan. Cook, covered, over medium-high heat until boiling. Reduce heat to low and add red pepper, black pepper and dry mustard. Simmer, uncovered, until sauce starts to thicken. Add margarine and stir until blended. Taste and adjust seasoning, if necessary. Serve as desired.

Yield: 2 cups or 16 (2-tablespoon) servings

1 serving contains:

Cal	Prot	Fat	Chol	Carb	Fib	Sodium
32kc	1gm	trace	0	7gm	trace	239mg

Herb-Margarine Sauce

Keep some in the refrigerator at all times. Spoon over chicken or fish before baking. It's delicious over savory-filled crepes and most steamed or baked vegetables.

3 tablespoons low-fat margarine

1 garlic clove, minced

1 tablespoon chopped fresh parsley

1/2 teaspoon dried-leaf thyme

1/8 teaspoon pepper

In a small saucepan, melt margarine over medium heat. Stir in garlic, parsley, thyme and pepper. Remove from heat; cover and let stand 4 to 5 minutes. Store in the refrigerator and melt before using.

Yield: 4 (1-tablespoon) servings

1 serving contains:

Cal	Prot	Fat	Chol	Carb	Fib	Sodium
39kc	trace	4gm	0	trace	trace	105mg

Basic White Sauce

Used in numerous dishes as a base for other sauces or to bind mixtures. Makes a good low-salt substitute for undiluted canned cream soup.

2 tablespoons all-purpose flour

1 tablespoon non-fat milk powder

1 cup skim milk

1/8 teaspoon salt

1/8 teaspoon white pepper

1/4 teaspoon imitation butter flavoring

Variations

Thin White Sauce: Using the recipe above, reduce flour to 1 tablespoon.
Mushroom Sauce: Add 1/2 cup chopped fresh sautéed mushrooms.
Tomato Sauce: Stir in 1/4 cup tomato paste.
Celery Sauce: Add 2 tablespoons finely chopped sautéed celery and 1/2 teaspoon celery salt.
Chicken Sauce: Add 1 teaspoon chicken bouillon granules.

In a jar with a lid, combine flour, powdered milk and skim milk; shake until completely dissolved. Pour into a medium-size saucepan and cook over medium heat, stirring constantly, until sauce thickens. Stir in salt, pepper and butter flavoring.

Yield: 1 cup or 4 (1/4-cup) servings

1 serving contains:

Cal	Prot	Fat	Chol	Carb	Fib	Sodium
40kc	3gm	trace	1mg	7gm	trace	99mg

Marinara Sauce

Keep an extra batch in the freezer.

3 garlic cloves, minced

1 cup chopped onion

3/4 cup chopped green bell pepper

1-3/4 cups water

1 (28-oz.) can crushed Italian tomatoes

1 (8-oz.) can tomato sauce

1 (6-oz.) can tomato paste

1-1/2 teaspoons Italian seasoning

1 teaspoon dried-leaf basil

1/2 teaspoon dried-leaf oregano

3 teaspoons sugar

1/8 teaspoon ground allspice

1 tablespoon chopped fresh parsley

1/2 teaspoon salt

1/8 teaspoon pepper

In a large cast-iron skillet or soup pot over medium-high heat, cook garlic, onion and green pepper in 1/4 cup water until tender. Pour into a food processor fitted with the metal blade or a food mill. Add tomatoes and process until puréed; strain out tomato seeds. Return vegetable purée to skillet or pot. Add tomato sauce, tomato paste, 1-1/2 cups water, Italian seasoning, basil, oregano, sugar, allspice, parsley, salt and pepper; cover and bring to a boil. Reduce heat to a simmer. Simmer, uncovered, about 2 hours or until sauce reaches desired thickness. Taste and adjust seasoning, if necessary. Spoon over chicken or fish before or after baking or broiling. Serve as a sauce with pasta.

Yield: About 6 cups or 12 (1/2-cup) servings

1 serving contains:

Cal	Prot	Fat	Chol	Carb	Fib	Sodium
43kc	2gm	trace	0	10gm	1gm	313mg

Mornay Sauce

Smooth, flavorful and no fat.

1 cup skim milk

2 tablespoons non-fat milk powder

2 tablespoons all-purpose flour

1/4 teaspoon salt

1/4 cup grated Parmesan cheese

1 teaspoon lemon juice

In a jar with a lid, combine skim milk, powdered milk, flour and salt; shake until completely dissolved. Pour into a small heavy saucepan. Cook over medium heat, stirring constantly, until sauce thickens; cook 2 minutes longer. Remove from heat and stir in cheese and lemon juice. Serve hot with vegetables or fish.

Yield: 1-1/2 cups or 12 (2-tablespoon) servings

1 serving contains:

Cal	Prot	Fat	Chol	Carb	Fib	Sodium
24kc	2gm	1gm	2mg	2gm	trace	94mg

Judy's Mushroom Sauce

Splendid over chicken or vegetables.

2 tablespoons low-fat margarine

1/2 cup sliced fresh mushrooms or 1 (4-oz.) can

1 tablespoon all-purpose flour

3/4 cup skimmed evaporated milk

1 teaspoon soy sauce

White pepper to taste

In a medium-size heavy saucepan, melt margarine over medium-high heat. Add mushrooms and sauté until tender. Reduce heat to medium. In a jar with a lid, combine flour and milk; shake until completely dissolved. Slowly add to mushrooms, stirring constantly. Cook 3 or 4 minutes, stirring frequently. Add soy sauce. Stir constantly until sauce thickens. Season with pepper. Spoon over baked chicken or poached fish.

Yield: 1-1/4 cups or 10 (2-tablespoon) servings

1 serving contains:

Cal	Prot	Fat	Chol	Carb	Fib	Sodium
29kc	2gm	1gm	1mg	3gm	trace	84mg

Orange Sauce

For a special dessert, serve with Apple Crepes, page 303.

1/2 cup sugar

1 teaspoon cornstarch

1/2 cup orange juice

1/4 teaspoon grated orange peel

1 tablespoon low-fat margarine

1 tablespoon orange liqueur

In a small saucepan, thoroughly combine sugar and cornstarch. Add orange juice and cook over medium heat, stirring constantly until sauce starts to thicken. Add orange peel, margarine and liqueur, stir until blended. Serve warm with your dessert of choice.

Yield: 3/4 cup or 6 (2-tablespoon) servings

1 serving contains:

Cal	Prot	Fat	Chol	Carb	Fib	Sodium
87kc	trace	1gm	0	20gm	trace	24mg

Sour-Cream Substitute

Base for a wide variety of cold sauces and dips.

1 cup low-fat cottage cheese

2 tablespoons plain low-fat yogurt

Put cottage cheese and yogurt in a blender; process until smooth. Cover and refrigerate until ready to use.

Yield: 1 cup or 8 (2-tablespoon) servings

1 serving contains:

Cal	Prot	Fat	Chol	Carb	Fib	Sodium
23kc	4gm	trace	1mg	1gm	0	117mg

Strawberry Sauce

Adds a special touch to Strawberry Crepes, page 305.

1 cup sugar

3-1/2 tablespoons cornstarch

1/2 cup water

1 teaspoon lemon juice

1/2 cup crushed strawberries

In a small saucepan, thoroughly combine sugar and cornstarch. Gradually stir in water, lemon juice and crushed strawberries. Stir over medium heat until boiling; cook about 3 minutes longer, then set aside to cool. Sauce thickens as it cools. Serve at desired temperature with dessert of choice.

Yield: 1-1/4 cups or 10 (2-tablespoon) servings

1 serving contains:

Cal	Prot	Fat	Chol	Carb	Fib	Sodium
85kc	trace	trace	0	22gm	trace	trace

Tart Lemon Sauce

Perks up any dish.

2 tablespoons low-fat margarine

1/4 teaspoon imitation butter flavoring

1 tablespoon lemon juice

1 tablespoon chopped fresh parsley

In a small saucepan, melt margarine over medium heat. Stir in imitation butter flavoring, lemon juice and parsley. Remove from heat; cover and let stand 4 to 5 minutes. Spoon over cooked fish or steamed vegetables.

Yield: 4 (1-tablespoon) servings

1 serving contains:

Cal	Prot	Fat	Chol	Carb	Fib	Sodium
26kc	trace	3gm	0	trace	trace	70mg

Chocolate Sauce

Delicious served as a fondue with fresh fruit or as a topping over Angel food cake.

2 cups sugar

7 tablespoons unsweetened cocoa

1-2/3 cups skimmed evaporated milk

1-1/2 teaspoons low-fat margarine

1 teaspoon vanilla extract

In a medium-size saucepan, mix sugar and cocoa well. Add milk and margarine; bring to a boil over medium-high heat, stirring constantly. Reduce heat to medium and cook 5 minutes longer, stirring frequently. Remove from heat. Add vanilla and beat vigorously 1 minute. Stir vigorously from time to time as sauce cools. Serve warm.

Yield: 2-1/3 cups or 18 (2-tablespoon) servings

1 serving contains:

Cal	Prot	Fat	Chol	Carb	Fib	Sodium
108kc	2gm	1gm	1mg	25gm	0	31mg

Vanilla Sauce

Finishing touch for Dutch Apple Cake, page 260.

1/4 cup sugar

1-1/2 teaspoons cornstarch

1/8 teaspoon ground nutmeg

1/2 cup boiling water

1/2 tablespoon low-fat margarine

1 teaspoon vanilla extract

In a small saucepan, thoroughly combine sugar, cornstarch and nutmeg. Slowly stir in boiling water and cook, stirring, over medium heat until sauce thickens; cook 1 minute longer. Remove from heat and stir in margarine and vanilla. Serve warm with your dessert of choice.

Yield: 3/4 cup or 6 (2-tablespoon) servings

1 serving contains:

Cal	Prot	Fat	Chol	Carb	Fib	Sodium
' 37kc	trace	trace	0	9gm	0	12mg

Lemon-Raisin Sauce

One of our family's favorites served over Gingerbread, page 268, or Dutch Apple Cake, page 260.

1/2 cup sugar

1 tablespoon cornstarch

1 cup boiling water

2 tablespoons lemon juice

1 teaspoon low-fat margarine

1/2 cup raisins

In a small saucepan, blend sugar and cornstarch, Gradually add water, stirring constantly over medium heat until boiling; boil 1 minute. Remove from heat and stir in lemon juice, margarine and raisins. Serve warm with your dessert of choice.

Yield: 9 (3-tablespoon) servings

1 serving contains:

Cal	Prot	Fat	Chol	Carb	Fib	Sodium
70kc	trace	trace	0	18gm	1gm	6mg

Sandwiches

When preparing sandwiches for your family or friends, be creative! Make the food as interesting and appealing as possible.

Use a wide variety of breads as the base for your sandwiches. Alternate between whole-wheat, rye, pumpernickel, sourdough, pita bread, English muffins and tortillas. Homemade Biscuits, page 66, are delicious when filled with your favorite chicken or tuna salad. Don't forget the wide assortment of crisp flatbreads, rice cakes and crackers. Always read labels to make sure the crackers are permissible on your diet.

What could be simpler for a nutritious sandwich than taking a small flour tortilla and adding a slice of low-fat cheese? Toast in the toaster oven, then when brown, fold in half. Serve with a cup of soup.

For a colorful assortment of garnishes, walk through the produce section of your grocery store and let your imagination run wild. Add sprouts to your favorite sandwich. Have you ever tried roasted bell peppers on a sandwich? Red or yellow bell peppers are especially delicious this way. Or use strips of roasted chile peppers for outstanding flavor. Try fresh spinach when you might normally use lettuce.

How about a combination of plain low-fat yogurt, low-fat

mayonnaise-type salad dressing, alfalfa sprouts and finely chopped cucumber added to a sliced turkey breast on pumpernickel sandwich? Or use the same mixture with chopped water chestnuts instead of cucumber.

Blend a little lemon thyme in your low-fat mayonnaise-type salad dressing, then let it stand a couple of hours to blend the flavors. It's great with poultry or fish sandwiches.

As you browse through this book, look for ideas that appeal to you. For a light but special sandwich lunch, try Crab Dip, page 35, served on fresh sourdough rolls with tomato slices and sprouts.

Chipped Turkey Sandwich

Barbecue sauce gives hearty flavor to this Super Bowl special.

2 lbs. cooked turkey white meat, sliced very thin

About 1 cup Grandma's Barbecue Sauce, page 234

10 French bread-type buns or hard rolls

Serving Suggestions:

Carrot sticks
Corn Chips, page 40
Lettuce
Pickles, dill or sweet
Pineapple-Rhubarb Pie,
    page 293

Preheat oven to 350F (175C). Chop turkey very fine. Place in a 2-quart shallow baking dish; pour desired amount of sauce over. Cover and heat in oven about 30 minutes, or microwave just until heated. Spoon onto buns and serve.

Yield: 10 servings

1 serving contains:

Cal	Prot	Fat	Chol	Carb	Fib	Sodium
538kc	40gm	5gm	76mg	81gm	trace	999mg

Cheesey Chicken Sandwich

A delicious blending of flavors.

3 whole chicken breasts, halved, skinned, boned

1/4 teaspoon salt

1/8 teaspoon lemon pepper

2 tablespoons all-purpose flour

1 teaspoon low-fat margarine

1/4 cup low-fat mayonnaise-type salad dressing

1/2 teaspoon dill weed

1/4 cup finely chopped green onion

1/3 cup shredded low-fat cheddar cheese

6 English muffins, halved, toasted

6 pineapple rings, drained, fresh or canned

Serving Suggestions:

Macaroni Salad, page 105
Best Oatmeal Cookies, page 273

Pound chicken breasts to flatten. Combine salt, lemon pepper and flour; use to dredge chicken pieces. Melt margarine in a large non-stick skillet over medium-high heat. Add chicken pieces and cook 15 to 20 minutes or until brown and tender. Preheat broiler. While chicken is cooking, combine salad dressing, dill, green onion and cheese in a small bowl. Lay halved muffins on a clean surface. Spread half of dressing mixture over muffins, then top each muffin half with a piece of chicken. Set a pineapple ring on top of chicken; spread remaining dressing mixture over all. Broil 3 to 4 minutes or until brown. Top with remaining muffin halves and serve.

Yield: 6 servings

1 serving contains:

Cal	Prot	Fat	Chol	Carb	Fib	Sodium
334kc	34gm	5gm	78mg	35gm	trace	566mg

Chicken-Curry Sandwich

Use leftovers for a delicious supper.

4 slices whole-wheat bread, toasted

8 slices cooked chicken white meat, about 1/3 lb.

4 thin slices cranberry sauce, about 3 oz.

1/3 cup low-fat mayonnaise-type salad dressing

1/4 cup minced celery

1/4 cup minced onion

Dash of curry powder

Serving Suggestions:

Joyce's Cream of Broccoli Soup, page 58
Sliced fresh fruit

Preheat broiler. Place toasted bread on a baking sheet; arrange 2 chicken slices on each piece. Lay cranberry slices on top of chicken. In a small bowl, combine salad dressing, celery and onion; spoon over cranberries. Sprinkle curry powder over all. Place under broiler and heat until bubbling and slightly brown. Serve immediately.

Yield: 4 servings

1 serving contains:

Cal	Prot	Fat	Chol	Carb	Fib	Sodium
183kc	14gm	5gm	29mg	23gm	3gm	254mg

Grilled-Chicken Sandwiches

The younger crowd loves these.

1 recipe Grilled Chicken with Herbs, page 140

1 tablespoon low-fat mayonnaise-type salad dressing

4 French bread-type rolls or hard rolls

Lettuce, tomato slices, pickles to garnish

Serving Suggestions:

Herb Dip with fresh veggies, page 34
Carolyn's Cauliflower Salad, page 102
Fresh Fruit Salad, page 90

Prepare Italian Grilled Chicken. Spread salad dressing over rolls. Set chicken on top, then garnish as desired and serve.

Yield: 4 servings

1 serving contains:

Cal	Prot	Fat	Chol	Carb	Fib	Sodium
384kc	34gm	8gm	75mg	39gm	1gm	660mg

Hot Puffy Chicken Sandwiches

You will like this unusual sandwich.

2 cups finely chopped cooked chicken white meat

1/2 cup finely chopped celery

1/3 cup low-fat mayonnaise-type salad dressing

1 tablespoon lemon juice

6 slices whole-wheat bread, toasted

3 egg whites

1/2 cup shredded low-fat cheddar cheese

1/8 teaspoon dill weed

Serving Suggestions:

Fresh-Fruit Salad, page 90
Gingerbread, page 268

Preheat broiler. In a medium-size bowl, combine chicken, celery, salad dressing and lemon juice. Place toasted bread on a baking sheet; spread chicken mixture on toast. In a large bowl, beat egg whites until stiff peaks form; gently fold in cheese and dill. Spread over chicken. Broil 8 to 10 minutes or until golden brown. Serve immediately.

Yield: 6 servings

1 serving contains:

Cal	Prot	Fat	Chol	Carb	Fib	Sodium
218kc	25gm	7gm	57mg	16gm	3gm	363mg

Salmon Burgers

A different, exciting sandwich.

1 recipe Salmon Patties, page 174

6 soft whole-wheat sandwich buns, halved

3 teaspoons brown mustard

Sweet-onion slices, sprouts to garnish

Serving Suggestions:

Sliced tomatoes and cucumbers
Joy's Pear-Crumble Pie, page 291

Prepare Salmon Patties, making 6 patties. Cook as directed; set aside. Lay buns on a clean surface. Spread mustard on bottom half of each bun and set a salmon patty on top. Garnish as desired and serve.

Yield: 6 servings

1 serving contains:

Cal	Prot	Fat	Chol	Carb	Fib	Sodium
299kc	20gm	8gm	31mg	34gm	1gm	752mg

Sloppy Joes

New twist for an old favorite.

1/4 cup finely chopped onion

1/4 cup finely chopped green bell pepper

2 tablespoons water

1 lb. raw ground turkey

1 cup Grandma's Barbecue Sauce, page 234

6 soft whole-wheat sandwich buns

Crisp sweet pickles to garnish

Serving Suggestions:

Oven French Fries, page 214
Applesauce Bars, page 261

In a large iron skillet or heavy saucepan over low heat, cook onion and green pepper in water until tender. Add ground turkey and cook, stirring often, until done and it has lost its pink color. Stir in sauce. Simmer, uncovered, about 30 minutes. Spoon onto buns and serve with pickles.

Yield: 6 servings

1 serving contains:

Cal	Prot	Fat	Chol	Carb	Fib	Sodium
381kc	14gm	4gm	32mg	28gm	trace	487mg

Soupy Chicken Sandwiches

Great supper for a cold winter night.

1 teaspoon low-fat margarine

1/2 cup thinly sliced green onion

1 (10-oz.) can cream of mushroom soup, not diluted, or Basic White Sauce with mushrooms, page 236

1/2 cup skim milk

1/4 teaspoon dill weed

2 cups finely chopped cooked chicken white meat

6 slices whole-wheat bread, toasted

6 slices tomato, about 4 oz.

6 slices low-fat cheddar cheese, 4-1/2 oz.

1/4 cup grated Parmesan cheese

Serving Suggestions:

Carrot sticks
Corn Chips, page 40
Chocolate Pudding, page 299

Preheat broiler. Melt margarine in a medium-size saucepan over medium-high heat. Add green onion and sauté until wilted. Stir in soup or sauce, milk and dill. Add chicken; stir gently until heated through. Place toasted bread on a baking sheet; arrange chicken mixture over toast. Set a tomato slice on top of each sandwich, then a slice of cheese. Sprinkle with Parmesan cheese. Broil 8 to 10 minutes or until lightly browned and bubbling.

Yield: 6 servings

1 serving contains:

Cal	Prot	Fat	Chol	Carb	Fib	Sodium
290kc	26gm	12gm	56mg	20gm	4gm	884mg

Desserts

Fresh fruit is the greatest natural dessert. However, there are times when we crave something else. This section was compiled to use when the craving is overwhelming. These desserts are lower in calories, saturated fat and cholesterol because they are made with poly-unsaturated oils and margarines, and less of them, plus less sugar. I used non-fat milk and only egg whites or egg substitute. There's not much salt, either.

Desserts made with sugars should be prepared only for very special occasions. Angel-food cake, fresh fruit, gelatin, sorbet and ices are good alternatives to high-calorie desserts.

Grapefruit with Honey

Yummy, quick and healthy.

1 grapefruit, cut in half

2 teaspoons honey

Fresh mint, chopped

Variation

Sprinkle with 1/8 teaspoon ground cinnamon instead of mint.
Sprinkle with 1 tablespoon oat bran before broiling.

Preheat oven to broil. Place grapefruit cut side up on a baking dish. Spoon honey into core, sprinkle with mint and broil lightly. Serve immediately.

Yield: 2 servings

1 serving contains:

Cal	Prot	Fat	Chol	Carb	Fib	Sodium
59kc	1gm	trace	0	15gm	2gm	trace

Cantaloupe Bowls

A refreshingly fresh dessert.

1 large ripe cantaloupe

2 pints fresh strawberries, washed, hulled

2 kiwi fruit, sliced

Fresh spearmint leaves

Cut cantaloupe in half and remove seeds. Cut edges in a saw-tooth design. Using a melon baller, remove melon flesh and place in a medium-size bowl. Add strawberries, kiwi and mint leaves. Toss gently, then spoon into the cantaloupe shells. Serve immediately.

Yield: 14 (1/2-cup) servings

1 serving contains:

Cal	Prot	Fat	Chol	Carb	Fib	Sodium
36kc	1gm	trace	0	8gm	2gm	5mg

Dutch Apple Cake

Serve warm with Vanilla Sauce,
page 245.

1 cup unbleached or
**   all-purpose flour, sifted**

5 tablespoons sugar

1 teaspoon baking powder

2 tablespoons low-fat margarine

2 egg whites, slightly beaten

1/4 cup skim milk

1/2 teaspoon vanilla extract

4 cups sliced, peeled apples

1 teaspoon ground cinnamon

Preheat oven to 375F (190C). Grease and flour a 9-inch tart or pie pan. In a mixing bowl, combine flour, 2 table-spoons sugar and baking powder. With a pastry blender or 2 knives, cut in 1-1/2 tablespoons margarine. Add egg whites, milk and vanilla; beat until smooth. Batter will be stiff. Spoon into prepared pan and spread batter to fit pan. Arrange apple slices, overlapping, in 2 concentric circles to cover batter. In a small bowl, combine 3 tablespoons sugar and cinnamon; sprinkle over apple slices. Dot with 1/2 tablespoon margarine. Bake 30 minutes. Cool 10 minutes before serving.

Yield: 6 servings

1 serving contains:

Cal	Prot	Fat	Chol	Carb	Fib	Sodium
183kc	4gm	2gm	trace	38gm	2gm	125mg

Applesauce Bars

A moist, cinnamony treat.

2 cups unbleached or
  all-purpose flour

1 teaspoon baking soda

1 teaspoon ground cinnamon

1 teaspoon ground nutmeg

1/2 teaspoon ground cloves

1/2 cup low-fat margarine,
  room temperature

1/2 cup firmly packed brown sugar

1/2 cup granulated sugar

2 egg whites, slightly beaten

1 cup unsweetened applesauce

1 cup raisins

Icing:

1 cup powdered sugar

2 tablespoons hot skim milk

1/2 teaspoon vanilla extract

1/4 teaspoon imitation butter
  flavoring

Preheat oven to 350F (175C). Lightly grease and flour a 13" x 9" baking pan. Sift flour, baking soda and spices into a medium-size bowl; set aside. In a large mixing bowl, beat margarine, brown sugar and granulated sugar until light and fluffy. Stir in egg whites and applesauce. Gradually add flour mixture, beating well after each addition. Fold in raisins. Pour into prepared pan. Bake 25 to 30 minutes or until a wooden pick comes out clean. Let cool until slightly warm; prepare Icing.

Icing:

In a medium-size bowl, mix powdered sugar, milk, vanilla and butter flavoring; beat until smooth. Drizzle over warm cake. Cool completely before cutting into bars.

Yield: 12 servings

1 serving with icing contains:

Cal	Prot	Fat	Chol	Carb	Fib	Sodium
256kc	3gm	4gm	trace	53gm	2gm	176mg

Banana Cake

Make a day ahead for a truly moist banana flavor. For special occasions, top with 7-Minute Frosting, page 272.

2-1/2 cups cake flour

1-2/3 cups sugar

1-1/4 teaspoons baking powder

1-1/4 teaspoons baking soda

1/3 cup low-fat margarine, room temperature

1/3 cup vegetable oil

1-1/4 cups mashed bananas, very ripe

2/3 cup sour skim milk

4 egg whites, slightly beaten

Preheat oven to 350F (175C). Grease and flour two (9-inch) cake pans or one (13" x 9") baking pan. Sift flour, sugar, baking powder and baking soda together into a large mixing bowl. Add shortening, bananas and half the milk; beat at medium speed 2 minutes. Add egg whites and remaining milk; beat 2 minutes longer. Pour into prepared pans. Bake 9-inch layers 35 minutes, 13" x 9" pan 45 to 50 minutes, or until a wooden pick comes out clean. Invert onto cooling racks. Let stand 10 minutes before removing pan. Cool completely before serving.

Yield: 12 servings

1 serving without frosting contains:

Cal	Prot	Fat	Chol	Carb	Fib	Sodium
296kc	4gm	9gm	trace	52gm	1gm	206mg

Blueberry Tea Cake

Perfect dessert for brunch.

**1/4 cup low-fat margarine,
room temperature**

3/4 cup sugar

2 egg whites, slightly beaten

1/2 cup skim milk

**2 cups unbleached or
all-purpose flour**

2 teaspoons baking powder

2 cups fresh or frozen blueberries

Topping:
1/2 cup sugar

**1/4 cup unbleached or
all-purpose flour**

1/2 teaspoon ground cinnamon

1/2 teaspoon ground nutmeg

1/4 teaspoon ground allspice

**2 tablespoons low-fat margarine,
room temperature**

Preheat oven to 375F (190C). Grease and flour a 9-inch-square baking pan. In a large mixing bowl, beat together margarine and sugar until light and fluffy. Add egg whites and milk; blend well. Sift together flour and baking soda into a medium-size bowl. Stir into margarine mixture. Fold in blueberries. Spoon into prepared pan.

Topping:

To make the topping, combine sugar, flour, cinnamon, nutmeg and allspice in a small bowl. Cut in margarine with a pastry blender. Sprinkle over cake batter. Bake 40 to 45 minutes or until a wooden pick comes out clean. Serve warm or cooled.

Yield: 9 servings

1 serving contains:

Cal	Prot	Fat	Chol	Carb	Fib	Sodium
276kc	5gm	4gm	trace	56gm	2gm	189mg

Caroline's Chocolate Cake

If you like chocolate cake, this will be your favorite.

1/2 cup low-fat margarine, room temperature

1-3/4 cups sugar

1-2/3 cups cold water

1/2 cup cocoa

1 teaspoon vanilla extract

2-1/2 cups sifted cake flour

3 egg whites

1-1/2 teaspoons soda

Preheat oven to 350F (175C). Grease and flour two (9-inch-square) or one (13" x 9") baking pan. In a large mixing bowl, beat margarine and 1 cup sugar until light and fluffy. Add 1/3 cup cold water, cocoa and vanilla, mixing well. Add flour alternately with 1 cup water, beating after each addition. In a mixing bowl, beat egg whites lightly; gradually add 3/4 cup sugar. Beat until stiff peaks form. Fold beaten egg whites into batter. Dissolve soda in remaining 1/3 cup water, stir into batter. Pour batter into prepared pans. Bake 9-inch layers 30 to 35 minutes, 13" x 9" pan 35 to 40 minutes, or until a wooden pick comes out clean. Invert onto cooling racks. Let stand 10 minutes before removing pan. Cool completely before frosting and serving.

Yield: 12 servings

1 serving without frosting contains:

Cal	Prot	Fat	Chol	Carb	Fib	Sodium
242kc	4gm	5gm	0	45gm	1gm	208mg

Johnny's Oatmeal Cake

So moist and yummy.

1 cup rolled oats, uncooked

1-1/4 cups boiling water

1/2 cup low-fat margarine, room temperature

1 cup white sugar

1 cup firmly packed brown sugar

1 teaspoon vanilla extract

3 egg whites, slightly beaten

1-1/2 cups unbleached or all-purpose flour

1 teaspoon baking soda

3/4 teaspoon ground cinnamon

1/4 teaspoon ground nutmeg

1/2 cup raisins

Frosting:
1 tablespoon low-fat margarine, melted

1 tablespoon brown sugar

1 tablespoon white sugar

1 tablespoon skim milk

1/2 teaspoon vanilla extract

Preheat oven to 350F (175C). Grease and flour a 9-inch-square baking pan. Place oats in a medium-size bowl. Pour boiling water over oats; cover and let stand 20 minutes. In a large mixing bowl, beat margarine and sugars until light and fluffy. Blend in vanilla and egg whites. Add oats mixture and mix well. Sift together flour, baking soda, cinnamon and nutmeg into a medium-size bowl. Add to oats mixture. Add raisins and mix well. Pour batter into prepared pan. Bake 50 to 55 minutes. Cool completely before frosting and serving.

Frosting:

Combine margarine, sugars and milk in a small saucepan. Bring to a boil and boil 1 minute. Stir in vanilla and spoon over cooled cake.

Yield: 9 servings

1 serving with frosting contains:

Cal	Prot	Fat	Chol	Carb	Fib	Sodium
373kc	5gm	7gm	0	76gm	2gm	257mg

Sewing-circle Favorite

Apple pieces and raisins give this cake a delightful texture.

1-3/4 cups sugar

3/4 cup oil of choice

4 egg whites, slightly beaten

2 cups unbleached or all-purpose flour

1 teaspoon baking soda

1 tablespoon ground cinnamon

1/8 teaspoon ground cloves

1 teaspoon ground nutmeg

5 large apples, peeled, cut into bite-size pieces (5 to 6 cups)

1 cup raisins

2 tablespoons powdered sugar

Preheat oven to 350F (175C). Lightly spray 13" x 9" baking pan with vegetable spray. In a large bowl, combine sugar and oil; stir in egg whites. Add flour, baking soda, cinnamon, cloves and nutmeg; mix well. Fold in apples and raisins. Spoon into prepared pan; batter will be thick. Bake 50 to 55 minutes or until a wooden pick comes out clean. Sift powdered sugar over cake while still warm. Cool before serving.

Yield: 12 servings

1 serving contains:

Cal	Prot	Fat	Chol	Carb	Fib	Sodium
378kc	4gm	14gm	0	63gm	3gm	88mg

Strawberry Shortcake

A delightful springtime dessert.

1-1/2 cups Baking Mix, page 65

1/2 cup sugar

2 egg whites, slightly beaten

1/2 cup water

1 teaspoon vanilla extract

2 quarts strawberries, hulled, rinsed

**1/2 cup sugar or
artificial sweetener to taste**

Preheat oven to 350F (175C). Lightly grease and flour an 8-inch-square baking pan. In a medium-size mixing bowl, combine Baking Mix, sugar, egg whites, water and vanilla; beat at low speed until moistened. Beat at medium speed 4 minutes, scraping sides of bowl occasionally. Pour into prepared pan. Bake 30 minutes or until a wooden pick comes out clean. Cool. While cake is baking, slice strawberries and sprinkle with sugar. Chill until ready to use. To serve, cut a square of cake, place in dessert dish and top with strawberries.

Yield: 9 servings

1 serving contains:

Cal	Prot	Fat	Chol	Carb	Fib	Sodium
194kc	3gm	3gm	trace	40gm	3gm	190mg

Gingerbread

Moist, spicy and delicious, top it with Lemon-Raisin Sauce, page 246.

1/2 cup oil of choice

2 tablespoons brown sugar

2 egg whites, slightly beaten

1 cup dark molasses

1 cup boiling water

2-1/4 cups unbleached or all-purpose flour

1 teaspoon baking soda

1 teaspoon ground ginger

1 teaspoon ground cinnamon

1/8 teaspoon ground allspice

Preheat oven to 350F (175C). Lightly grease and flour an 8-inch-square baking pan. In a large bowl, combine oil, sugar and egg whites. Stir in molasses and water. Sift together flour, baking soda, ginger, cinnamon and allspice into a medium-size bowl. Stir into molasses mixture. Pour into prepared pan. Bake 45 to 50 minutes. Cool before serving.

Yield: 9 servings

1 serving contains:

Cal	Prot	Fat	Chol	Carb	Fib	Sodium
317kc	4gm	12gm	0	47gm	1gm	136mg

Pineapple-Cherry Upside-Down Cake

One of my childhood favorites.

2 tablespoons low-fat margarine

1/2 cup firmly packed brown sugar

6 canned pineapple slices

6 maraschino cherries

1 cup cake flour, sifted

3/4 cup sugar

1/4 cup oil of choice

1/2 cup skim milk

1-1/2 teaspoons baking powder

3 egg whites, slightly beaten

1/2 teaspoon vanilla extract

Preheat oven to 350F (175C). In a round or square 8-inch baking pan, melt margarine; sprinkle with brown sugar. Arrange pineapple slices evenly around pan, then place a cherry in the center of each slice. In a large mixing bowl, combine flour and sugar. Blend in oil and 1/4 cup milk; beat 2 minutes. Stir in baking powder, remaining milk, egg whites and vanilla; beat at medium speed 2 minutes longer. Pour batter over pineapple. Bake 35 to 40 minutes or until a wooden pick comes out clean. Immediately invert onto a serving plate; leave pan over cake about 5 minutes, then remove. Serve warm or cooled.

Yield: 8 servings

1 serving contains:

Cal	Prot	Fat	Chol	Carb	Fib	Sodium
284kc	3gm	9gm	trace	50gm	1gm	130mg

White Cake

You'll find many uses for this cake.

2 cups cake flour

1-1/2 cups sugar

1/2 cup oil of choice

1 cup skim milk

1 tablespoon baking powder

4 egg whites, slightly beaten

1 teaspoon vanilla extract

Preheat oven to 350F (175C). Grease and flour a 13" x 9" baking pan or two round 9-inch pans. Into a large mixing bowl, sift flour and sugar. Add oil and 1/4 cup milk. Beat 2 minutes on medium speed. Stir in baking powder, remaining milk and egg whites. Beat 2 minutes longer; stir in vanilla. Pour into prepared pan. Bake 30 to 35 minutes for 13" x 9" pan or 25 to 30 minutes for 9-inch pans.

Yield: 12 servings

1 serving without frosting contains:

Cal	Prot	Fat	Chol	Carb	Fib	Sodium
254kc	4gm	9gm	trace	40gm	1gm	113mg

Springfield Frosting

A light and creamy frosting.

**2-1/2 tablespoons unbleached or
all-purpose flour**

1/2 cup skim milk

1/2 cup low-fat margarine

1/2 cup powdered sugar

1 teaspoon vanilla extract

In a small saucepan, blend flour and milk together; stir over medium heat until thickened. Set aside to cool. In a mixer, beat margarine and powdered sugar until creamy. Add vanilla then flour-and-milk mixture. Beat until creamy and smooth. Use to frost cake of choice. Frosting may be stored several days in the refrigerator.

Yield: 12 servings, will frost a 13" x 9" cake

1 serving contains:

Cal	Prot	Fat	Chol	Carb	Fib	Sodium
59kc	1gm	4gm	trace	6gm	trace	98mg

7-Minute Frosting

An easy, reliable frosting.

2 egg whites

1-1/4 cups sugar

1/2 teaspoon cream of tartar

1 tablespoon light corn syrup

1/3 cup water

1-1/2 teaspoons vanilla extract

In the bottom of a double boiler, bring about 1 cup water to a boil. In double boiler top, combine egg whites, sugar, cream of tartar, syrup and water. Set top pan over boiling water on medium heat. Beat mixture with an electric mixer on high speed until mixture holds a stiff peak. Add vanilla and blend in. Use to frost cooled cake of choice.

Yield: 12 servings, will frost a 13" x 9" cake

1 serving contains:

Cal	Prot	Fat	Chol	Carb	Fib	Sodium
83kc	1gm	0	0	21gm	0	10mg

Best Oatmeal Cookies

The name says it all.

3/4 cup low-fat margarine, room temperature

1 cup white sugar

1/2 cup firmly packed brown sugar

2 egg whites, slightly beaten

1-1/2 cups unbleached or all-purpose flour

1 teaspoon baking soda

1 teaspoon ground cinnamon

1/4 teaspoon ground nutmeg

1-1/2 cups oats, uncooked

1 cup raisins

1 teaspoon vanilla extract

In a large mixing bowl, beat margarine and sugars until light and fluffy. Add egg whites. In a medium-size bowl, combine flour, baking soda, cinnamon and nutmeg; add to sugar mixture. Stir in oats, raisins and vanilla. Chill 1 hour. Preheat oven to 350F (175C). Roll a teaspoon of dough into a ball and place on an ungreased cookie sheet. Grease the bottom of a glass with margarine, dip glass in sugar and use to flatten ball of dough. Continue until cookie sheet is full, leaving adequate space between cookies. Bake 10 minutes. Cool on wire racks.

Yield: About 55 cookies

1 cookie contains:

Cal	Prot	Fat	Chol	Carb	Fib	Sodium
61kc	1gm	1gm	0	12gm	trace	48mg

Date Pinwheels

Freeze the cookie-dough rolls so you can slice and bake as needed.

Filling:

1 (7-1/4 oz.) pkg. dates, chopped

1/3 cup water

1/4 cup sugar

Dough:

1/3 cup low-fat margarine, room temperature

1/2 cup firmly packed brown sugar

1/2 cup granulated sugar

1/2 teaspoon vanilla extract

2 egg whites, slightly beaten

2 cups unbleached or all-purpose flour

1/4 teaspoon baking soda

Filling:
In a medium-size saucepan, combine dates, water and sugar. Bring to a boil and simmer for 5 minutes, stirring often. Set aside to cool.

Dough:
In a large mixing bowl, beat margarine, brown sugar and granulated sugar until light and fluffy. Add vanilla and egg whites; mix well. In a medium-size bowl, combine dry ingredients; add to creamed mixture and mix well. Refrigerate until firm enough to roll. Cut dough in half. On a floured surface, roll each half into a 12" x 9" rectangle; spread with filling. Roll up tightly, jelly-roll fashion. Cover with foil or plastic wrap. Refrigerate overnight or freeze. To cook, preheat oven to 375F (190C). Lightly spray a cookie sheet with vegetable spray. Cut chilled dough into 1/8-inch-thick slices; place on prepared cookie sheeet. Bake 10 minutes. Cool on wire racks.

Yield: 50 pinwheels

1 pinwheel contains:

Cal	Prot	Fat	Chol	Carb	Fib	Sodium
54kc	1gm	1gm	0	12gm	trace	22mg

English Teacakes

A nice little dessert, yet not too sweet.

**1-3/4 cups unbleached or
all-purpose flour**

1-1/2 teaspoons baking powder

**1/2 cup low-fat margarine,
room temperature**

1 cup sugar

3 egg whites, slightly beaten

3 tablespoons skim milk

1/2 cup chopped candied fruit

1/2 cup raisins

In a medium-size bowl, mix flour and baking powder. In a large mixing bowl, beat margarine, 3/4 cup sugar and 2 egg whites until smooth. Add milk and flour mixture alternately, mixing well after each addition. Stir in candied fruit and raisins; mix well. Refrigerate at least 1 hour. Preheat oven to 400F (205C). Lightly spray a cookie sheet with vegetable spray. Place 1/4 cup sugar in a shallow bowl. Roll dough into walnut-size balls, dip the top of each ball into remaining egg white, then into sugar. Place on prepared cookie sheet. Bake 12 to 15 minutes or until golden brown. Cool on wire racks.

Yield: 55 cookies

1 cookie contains:

Cal	Prot	Fat	Chol	Carb	Fib	Sodium
45kc	1gm	1gm	trace	9gm	trace	34mg

Betty's Apple Cookies

Wonderfully moist and flavorful.

2 cups unbleached or all-purpose flour

1 teaspoon baking soda

1 teaspoon ground cloves

1/2 teaspoon ground cinnamon

1/2 teaspoon ground nutmeg

1/2 cup low-fat margarine, room temperature

1-1/3 cups firmly packed brown sugar

2 egg whites, slightly beaten

1/4 cup apple juice or water

1 cup finely chopped apples

1 cup raisins

Preheat oven to 350F (175C). Lightly spray a cookie sheet with vegetable spray. In a medium bowl, mix flour, baking soda, cloves, cinnamon and nutmeg. In a large mixing bowl, beat margarine and sugar until light and fluffy. Add egg whites, then juice or water, stirring to mix well. Add dry ingredients gradually; fold in apples and raisins. Drop by teaspoonfuls onto prepared cookie sheet. Bake 12 to 15 minutes. Cool on wire racks.

Yield: 60 cookies

1 cookie contains:

Cal	Prot	Fat	Chol	Carb	Fib	Sodium
50kc	1gm	1gm	0	10gm	trace	36mg

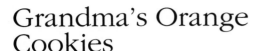
Grandma's Orange Cookies

Smooth texture and orange flavor bring back special memories.

4-1/2 cups unbleached or all-purpose flour

1 teaspoon baking soda

2 teaspoons baking powder

3/4 cup low-fat margarine, room temperature

2 cups sugar

4 egg whites, slightly beaten

1 cup orange juice

1 tablespoon grated orange peel

1 cup sour skim milk

Orange Cookie Icing, page 282

Preheat oven to 350F (175C). Lightly spray a cookie sheet with vegetable spray. In a medium bowl mix flour, baking soda and baking powder. In a large mixing bowl, beat margarine and sugar until light and fluffy. Add egg whites, juice and orange peel. Alternating flour mixture with sour milk, mix thoroughly. Drop by teaspoonfuls onto prepared cookie sheet. Bake 8 minutes or until set. Cool on wire racks. Ice if desired.

Yield: About 90 cookies

1 cookie without icing contains:

Cal	Prot	Fat	Chol	Carb	Fib	Sodium
48kc	1gm	1gm	trace	9gm	trace	39mg

1 cookie with icing contains:

Cal	Prot	Fat	Chol	Carb	Fib	Sodium
57kc	1gm	1gm	trace	11gm	trace	40mg

Holiday Fruit Cookies

So easy to make and they freeze well, too.

1 cup low-fat margarine, room temperature

2 cups firmly packed brown sugar

3 egg whites, slightly beaten

1/2 cup sour skim milk

3-1/2 cups unbleached or all-purpose flour

1 teaspoon baking soda

2 cups chopped candied fruit

2 cups chopped dates

Preheat oven to 400F (205C). Lightly spray a cookie sheet with vegetable spray. In a large mixing bowl, beat margarine, sugar and egg whites. Stir in sour milk. Gradually add flour and baking soda; mix well. Fold in fruit. Drop by teaspoonfuls onto prepared cookie sheet. Bake 8 to 10 minutes or until set. Cool on wire racks.

Yield: 85 cookies

1 cookie contains:

Cal	Prot	Fat	Chol	Carb	Fib	Sodium
73kc	1gm	1gm	trace	16gm	1gm	44mg

Orange Granola Cookies

So yummy and nutritious.

1/2 cup low-fat margarine, room temperature

1/2 cup sugar

2 egg whites, slightly beaten

1/2 cup honey

1/3 cup frozen orange-juice concentrate

2-1/4 cups unbleached or all-purpose flour

2-1/2 teaspoons baking powder

1/2 teaspoon baking soda

2 teaspoons ground cinnamon

1/4 teaspoon ground cloves

1 cup oats, uncooked

1 cup raisins

Preheat oven to 350F (175C). Lightly spray a cookie sheet with vegetable spray. In a large mixing bowl, beat margarine and sugar until light and fluffy. Beat in egg whites. Combine honey and orange juice in a small bowl; set aside. In a medium-size bowl, combine flour, baking powder, baking soda, cinnamon and cloves. Gradually add flour mixture to margarine mixture, alternating with honey mixture. Stir in oats and raisins. Drop by teaspoonfuls onto prepared cookie sheet. Bake about 12 minutes or until firm to the touch. Cool on wire racks.

Yield: 50 cookies

1 cookie contains:

Cal	Prot	Fat	Chol	Carb	Fib	Sodium
65kc	1gm	1gm	0	13gm	trace	50mg

Pineapple Cookies

Moist texture and tangy flavor.

**2/3 cup low-fat margarine,
room temperature**

**1-1/4 cups firmly packed brown
sugar**

3 egg whites, slightly beaten

**3/4 cup crushed pineapple,
well-drained**

1 teaspoon vanilla extract

**2 cups unbleached or
all-purpose flour**

1-1/2 teaspoons baking powder

1/4 teaspoon baking soda

Vanilla Cookie Icing, page 283

Preheat oven to 350F (175C). Lightly spray a cookie sheet with vegetable spray. In a large mixing bowl, beat margarine and sugar until light and fluffy. Add egg whites and beat well. Stir in pineapple and vanilla. In a medium-size bowl, combine flour, baking powder and baking soda. Gradually add flour mixture to creamed mixture, beating after each addition, until smooth. Drop by teaspoonfuls onto prepared cookie sheet. Bake 10 minutes or until done. Cool on wire racks.

Yield: 50 cookies

1 cookie contains:

Cal	Prot	Fat	Chol	Carb	Fib	Sodium
52kc	1gm	1gm	0	9gm	trace	48mg

1 cookie with icing contains:

Cal	Prot	Fat	Chol	Carb	Fib	Sodium
62kc	1gm	1gm	trace	11gm	trace	49mg

Pumpkin Cookies

Great flavor combination!

**2 cups unbleached or
all-purpose flour**

1 teaspoon baking soda

1 teaspoon baking powder

1/8 teaspoon ground cloves

1 teaspoon ground cinnamon

1 cup sugar

**3/4 cup low-fat margarine,
room temperature**

2 egg whites, slightly beaten

1 cup mashed, cooked pumpkin

1 teaspoon vanilla extract

1 cup chopped dates

**Brown-Sugar Cookie Icing,
page 284**

Preheat oven to 350F (175C). Lightly spray a cookie sheet with vegetable spray. In a medium-size bowl, combine flour, baking soda, baking powder, cloves and cinnamon. In a large mixing bowl, beat sugar and margarine until light and fluffy. Add egg whites, pumpkin and vanilla. Gradually stir in flour mixture; mix well. Fold in dates. Drop by teaspoonfuls onto prepared cookie sheet. Bake 10 to 12 minutes. Cool on wire racks. Ice if desired.

Yield: 60 cookies

1 cookie contains:

Cal	Prot	Fat	Chol	Carb	Fib	Sodium
47kc	1gm	1gm	0	9gm	trace	49mg

1 cookie with icing contains:

Cal	Prot	Fat	Chol	Carb	Fib	Sodium
61kc	1gm	1gm	trace	12gm	trace	52mg

Orange Cookie Icing

Refreshing light flavor complements most cookies.

2 cups powdered sugar

1 teaspoon low-fat margarine, room temperature

1/2 teaspoon orange flavoring

3 tablespoons skimmed evaporated milk

1 tablespoon grated orange peel

In a small bowl, mix sugar, margarine, orange flavoring, milk and peel; beat until smooth. Spread icing on each cookie; let set until firm.

Yield: Icing for 90 cookies

1 serving contains:

Cal	Prot	Fat	Chol	Carb	Fib	Sodium
9kc	trace	trace	trace	2gm	0	1mg

Vanilla Cookie Icing

Enchances a variety of cookies.

1-1/2 cups powdered sugar

1 teaspoon low-fat margarine, room temperature

1/2 teaspoon vanilla

2-1/2 tablespoons skim milk

1/8 teaspoon imitation butter flavoring

In a small bowl combine sugar, margarine, vanilla, butter flavoring and milk; beat until smooth. Spread icing over each cookie.

Yield: Icing for 60 cookies

1 serving contains:

Cal	Prot	Fat	Chol	Carb	Fib	Sodium
10kc	trace	trace	trace	2gm	0	1mg

Brown-Sugar Cookie Icing

A nice change in taste.

1 tablespoon low-fat margarine, room temperature

1/4 cup skim milk

1/2 cup firmly packed brown sugar

2 cups powdered sugar, sifted

1 teaspoon vanilla extract

In a medium-size saucepan combine margarine, milk and brown sugar; boil 2 minutes. Remove from heat and stir in powdered sugar and vanilla; beat until smooth. Add more powdered sugar or milk if needed to make it spreading consistency. Spread icing over each cookie.

Yield: Icing for 60 cookies

1 serving contains:

Cal	Prot	Fat	Chol	Carb	Fib	Sodium
21kc	trace	trace	trace	5gm	0	3mg

Apples & Cranberries

A favorite dessert for fall!

4 cups chopped, peeled apples

3 cups cranberries, washed, drained

1-1/2 cups granulated sugar

1/2 cup firmly packed brown sugar

1-1/2 cups oats, uncooked

**1/3 cup unbleached or
all-purpose flour**

1/2 teaspoon ground cinnamon

1/4 teaspoon ground cloves

1/2 cup low-fat margarine, melted

Preheat oven to 350F (175C). In a large bowl, combine apples, cranberries and granulated sugar. Spread in a shallow 2-quart casserole or a 10-inch-square pan. In a medium-size bowl, blend brown sugar, oatmeal, flour and spices. Pour melted margarine over oatmeal mixture; blend well. Spread topping over fruit. Bake, uncovered, 1 hour. Serve warm.

Yield: 10 servings

1 serving contains:

Cal	Prot	Fat	Chol	Carb	Fib	Sodium
291kc	2gm	6gm	0	61gm	1gm	115mg

Variation

Add 1/3 cup pecans with the crumb topping if your diet permits.

Blueberry & Peach Crisp

Nice dessert for a patio meal. Nectarines can be substituted for peaches.

2 medium peaches, peeled, sliced, about 1-1/4 cup

1 cup fresh or frozen blueberries

1/2 cup unbleached or all-purpose flour

1/2 cup firmly packed brown sugar

1 tablespoon low-fat margarine, room temperature

Preheat oven to 350F (175C). Place peach slices in a 9-inch pie plate; top with blueberries. In a small bowl, blend flour, sugar and margarine with a pastry blender until crumbly; sprinkle over fruit. Bake, uncovered, 30 minutes or until bubbling and brown. Serve warm.

Yield: 6 servings

1 serving contains:

Cal	Prot	Fat	Chol	Carb	Fib	Sodium
143kc	1gm	1gm	0	33gm	2gm	30mg

Cherry Cobbler

Cinnamon enchances the cherry flavor.

2 (21-oz.) cans cherry pie filling

1/2 teaspoon ground cinnamon

**1 cup unbleached or
    all-purpose flour**

1 tablespoon sugar

1 teaspoon baking powder

Pinch of ground ginger

1/2 cup skim milk

3-1/2 tablespoons oil of choice

Preheat oven to 400F (205C). Spoon pie filling into a shallow 2-quart baking dish; sprinkle with cinnamon. In a small bowl, combine flour, sugar, baking powder, ginger, milk and oil. Drop by teaspoonfuls onto pie filling. Bake, uncovered, 30 minutes or until nicely browned. Serve warm.

Yield: 12 servings

1 serving contains:

Cal	Prot	Fat	Chol	Carb	Fib	Sodium
211kc	2gm	4gm	trace	44gm	1gm	41mg

Grandma's Fruit Rings

Fresh peaches or apples are best in this old family favorite.

1-1/2 cups sugar

1-1/2 cups water

2-1/4 cups Baking Mix, page 65

2/3 cup water

2-1/2 cups finely chopped, peeled fruit

1/2 teaspoon ground cinnamon

Preheat oven to 350F (175C). In a small saucepan, combine sugar and water; heat until sugar dissolves. Pour into a shallow 10-inch-square baking dish. In a large bowl, combine Baking Mix and water; stir until a soft dough forms. Turn out onto a floured pastry sheet and roll into a 12-inch square. Scatter fruit over dough; sprinkle with cinnamon. Roll up dough jelly-roll style. Using a sharp knife, cut into 10 slices. Lay cut side up in pan with syrup. Bake 45 minutes. Serve warm.

Yield: 10 servings

1 serving with apples contains:

Cal	Prot	Fat	Chol	Carb	Fib	Sodium
211kc	2gm	2gm	trace	47gm	1gm	229mg

Peach Torte

Delicious with hot tea.

**1-1/4 cups plus 1 tablespoon
unbleached or all-purpose flour**

3/4 cup sugar

1/4 teaspoon baking powder

1 egg white, slightly beaten

**1/4 cup plus 1 tablespoon low-fat
margarine, room temperature**

2 tablespoons skim milk

**4 large peaches, peeled, sliced,
about 3 cups**

3/4 teaspoon ground cinnamon

Preheat oven to 400F (205C). In a large
bowl, combine 1-1/4 cups flour, 1/4 cup
sugar and baking powder. Add egg
white, 1/4 cup margarine and 2 tablespoons milk; mix well. Spoon into a
9-inch cake pan, pressing around bottom and edges. Arrange peach slices on
top of crust. In a small bowl, combine 1
tablespoon flour, 1/2 cup sugar and cinnamon. Sprinkle over fruit. Dot with 1
tablespoon margarine. Bake 15 minutes;
reduce heat to 350F (175C) and bake 30
minutes longer. Serve warm or cooled.

Yield: 4 servings

1 serving contains:

Cal	Prot	Fat	Chol	Carb	Fib	Sodium
392kc	6gm	8gm	trace	78gm	3gm	212mg

Baked Pears & Raisins

New twist for an old standby. Top with Whipped Topping, page 304, or low-fat ice milk.

1/2 cup fresh bread crumbs

1/4 cup oat bran

1/3 cup firmly packed brown sugar

1/4 teaspoon ground cinnamon

1/8 teaspoon ground nutmeg

1 egg white

4 firm ripe pears, peeled, cut in half, cored

1/2 cup raisins

1/4 cup water

Preheat oven to 350F (175C). In a small bowl, combine bread crumbs, oat bran, sugar, cinnamon and nutmeg; set aside. In a small mixing bowl, beat egg white. Dip pear halves in beaten egg white then in bread crumbs. Arrange pears in a 10-inch square baking pan. Spoon raisins into cavities of pears. Pour water gently into pan. Bake, uncovered, 40 minutes or until tender. Serve warm.

Yield: 8 servings

1 serving contains:

Cal	Prot	Fat	Chol	Carb	Fib	Sodium
148kc	3gm	1gm	0	35gm	4gm	57mg

Joy's Pear-Crumble Pie

Pears and lemon peel give a nice smooth flavor.

6 medium pears, peeled, sliced, 6 to 7 cups

3 tablespoons lemon juice

1/3 cup sugar

2 tablespoons unbleached or all-purpose flour

1/8 teaspoon ground cinnamon

1 teaspoon grated lemon peel

1 (9-inch) unbaked pastry shell, page 295

Topping:
1/2 cup unbleached or all-purpose flour

1/2 cup sugar

1/2 teaspoon ground ginger

1/2 teaspoon ground cinnamon

1/4 cup low-fat margarine, room temperature

Preheat oven to 400F (205C). Place pears in a large bowl; sprinkle with lemon juice. In a small bowl, combine sugar, flour, cinnamon and lemon peel. Sprinkle over sliced pears, tossing gently to coat. Spoon pear filling into pastry shell; set aside.

Topping:

In a medium-size bowl, combine topping ingredients. Blend with a pastry blender until crumbly. Sprinkle crumbs over pears. Bake 45 minutes or until pears are tender. Serve warm.

Yield: 8 servings

1 serving contains:

Cal	Prot	Fat	Chol	Carb	Fib	Sodium
344kc	4gm	11gm	trace	60gm	4gm	134mg

Fresh Peach Pie

A mouth-watering, summer treat with either peaches or apricots.

Dough for a 9-inch double-crust pie, page 295

4 cups fresh peaches, peeled and sliced

2 tablespoons lemon juice

1-1/4 cups sugar

1/2 cup unbleached or all-purpose flour

1/4 teaspoon ground nutmeg

1 teaspoon grated lemon peel

1/2 teaspoon low-fat margarine, room temperature

1/2 teaspoon sugar

Roll out and fit half of dough in a 9-inch pie pan. Preheat oven to 400F (205C). Place sliced peaches in a large bowl. Drizzle lemon juice over peaches and toss gently. In a small bowl, combine 1-1/4 cups sugar, flour, nutmeg and lemon peel; mix well. Sprinkle over peaches, tossing gently to coat. Spoon peaches into pie shell. Roll out remaining dough to fit pie. Place over peaches; make a slit in top crust. Spread margarine over top crust and sprinkle with 1/2 teaspoon sugar. Bake 50 minutes or until brown and bubbling. Serve warm.

Yield: 8 servings

1 serving contains:

Cal	Prot	Fat	Chol	Carb	Fib	Sodium
448kc	5gm	16gm	trace	73gm	3gm	132mg

Pineapple-Rhubarb Pie

Blending two distinct flavors creates an unusually good taste.

Dough for a 9-inch double-crust pie, page 295

1-1/2 cups sugar

1 tablespoon cornstarch

5 tablespoons unbleached or all-purpose flour

3 cups rhubarb, cut in small bite-size pieces

1-1/2 cups crushed pineapple with juice

1 teaspoon low-fat margarine

Roll out and fit half of dough in a 9-inch pie pan. Preheat oven to 450F (230C). Drain off 1/4 cup juice from pineapple; set aside for another use. In a small bowl, combine sugar, cornstarch and flour; blend well. Place rhubarb and crushed pineapple in a large bowl. Pour sugar mixture over fruit and toss gently to coat well. Spoon fruit into pie shell; dot with margarine. Roll out remaining dough to fit pie. Place over fruit filling; make slit in top crust. Bake 10 minutes; reduce heat to 375F (190C) and bake 25 minutes longer or until pastry is brown and filling is bubbling. Serve warm.

Yield: 8 servings

1 serving contains:

Cal	Prot	Fat	Chol	Carb	Fib	Sodium
451kc	5gm	16gm	trace	74gm	2gm	135mg

Strawberry & Rhubarb Pie

A perfect springtime dessert.

Dough for a 9-inch double-crust pie, page 295

2 cups fresh strawberries, cut in quarters

2 cups diced rhubarb

1-1/2 cups sugar

5 tablespoons cornstarch

1 teaspoon low-fat margarine

Roll out and fit half of dough in a 9-inch pie pan. Preheat oven to 400F (205C). In a large bowl, combine strawberries and rhubarb. In a small bowl, combine sugar and cornstarch; sprinkle over fruit, tossing gently to coat. Spoon fruit mixture into pie shell; dot with margarine. Roll out remaining dough to fit pie. Place over fruit filling; make slit in top crust. Bake 45 to 50 minutes or until brown and bubbling. Serve warm.

Yield: 8 servings

1 serving contains:

Cal	Prot	Fat	Chol	Carb	Fib	Sodium
441kc	4gm	16gm	trace	72gm	2gm	136mg

Pie Crust with Oil

A nice flaky crust.

**2-1/4 cups unbleached or
all-purpose flour**

1/2 teaspoon salt, optional

1/3 cup very cold skim milk

**1/2 cup plus 1 tablespoon oil of
choice, chilled**

Place flour and salt in a large bowl. Combine milk and oil; pour all at once into flour. Mix gently with a fork until blended. Divide dough in half. Place one half between two sheets of wax paper; refrigerate remaining dough. Roll out gently until desired size. Gently lift dough and paper; place paper-side up in pie pan. Remove paper, fit crust into pan. Repeat with second half of dough. Leave unbaked for fruit pies and proceed with fruit-pie recipe. For a baked crust, prick crust with a fork. Bake in a 475F (245C) oven 8 to 10 minutes or until golden brown.

Yield: 2 (9-inch) pie crusts or 16 (3-1/2-inch) servings

1 serving contains:

Cal	Prot	Fat	Chol	Carb	Fib	Sodium
134kc	2gm	8gm	trace	14gm	trace	64mg

Lemon Snow Pudding

Wonderfully light and refreshing.

3/4 cup sugar

1 tablespoon unflavored gelatin

1-1/4 cups water

1/4 cup lemon juice

2 egg whites, stiffly beaten

Ground nutmeg

3 thin lemon slices, halved

In a medium saucepan, combine sugar, gelatin and water. Cook over medium heat, stirring constantly until mixture starts to boil. Remove from heat and add lemon juice. Place pan in a bowl of cold water and cool until mixture begins to gel. In a large mixing bowl, beat egg whites until stiff peaks form. Gradually add gelatin mixture, stirring slowly until blended. Spoon into custard cups; chill until firm. To serve, dust lightly with nutmeg and garnish with lemon slices.

Yield: 6 servings

1 serving contains:

Cal	Prot	Fat	Chol	Carb	Fib	Sodium
108kc	3gm	trace	0	26gm	trace	20mg

Rice Pudding

Smooth and nourishing.

2 cups cooked rice

2 cups skim milk

1 tablespoon non-fat powdered milk

1/3 cup sugar

1/2 teaspoon low-fat margarine

1 cup raisins

1 teaspoon vanilla extract

In a medium-size saucepan, combine rice, milk, powdered milk, sugar and margarine. Cook over medium heat, stirring often, about 25 minutes or until most of liquid is absorbed. Stir in raisins. Continue cooking until liquid is absorbed. Add vanilla. Serve hot or cold in individual bowls, garnish with your favorite fresh-fruit sauce.

Yield: 8 servings

1 serving contains:

Cal	Prot	Fat	Chol	Carb	Fib	Sodium
155kc	4gm	trace	1mg	36gm	2gm	41mg

Pineapple Bavarian

So refreshing for a hot summer day

1 (0.6-oz.) box sugar-free lemon gelatin

2 cups boiling water

1 cup cold water

8 oz. plain low-fat yogurt

2 cups crushed pineapple and juice

1 small banana, cut into small cubes

In a medium-size bowl, combine gelatin and boiling water, stirring until completely dissolved. Stir in cold water. Refrigerate until gelatin begins to thicken. Add yogurt, beating at medium speed until well blended and fluffy. Fold in pineapple and banana. Spoon into sherbet glasses or a mold. Refrigerate until set. Serve chilled.

Yield: 12 servings

1 serving contains:

Cal	Prot	Fat	Chol	Carb	Fib	Sodium
40kc	2gm	trace	1mg	7gm	trace	54mg

Chocolate Pudding

No special ingredients are required for this old favorite.

3/4 cup sugar

1/4 cup cornstarch

1/4 cup cocoa powder

2-1/4 cups skim milk

2 tablespoons low-fat margarine

1 teaspoon vanilla extract

In a medium-size saucepan, combine sugar, cornstarch and cocoa; stir until cornstarch is well blended. Slowly stir in milk until well mixed. Cook over medium heat, stirring constantly until mixture thickens and boils; boil 1 minute. Remove from heat. Stir in margarine and vanilla. Pour into 4 individual serving dishes. Lay a piece of wax paper over each pudding to prevent a film from forming. Serve warm or chilled.

Yield: 4 servings

1 serving contains:

Cal	Prot	Fat	Chol	Carb	Fib	Sodium
256kc	5gm	5gm	2mg	53gm	0	137mg

Vanilla Pudding

Try serving this with a fruit salad.

2-1/4 cups skim milk

1/2 cup plus 1 tablespoon sugar

1/4 cup cornstarch

1/4 cup egg substitute

1 egg white, slightly beaten

2 tablespoons low-fat margarine

1 teaspoon vanilla extract

Pour milk into a medium-size saucepan; set over medium heat. While milk is heating, combine sugar and cornstarch in a small bowl; add egg substitute and egg white. When milk is warm, stir about 1/2 cup milk into sugar mixture, then slowly add that to remaining milk in pan. Cook over medium heat, stirring constantly until mixture thickens and boils; boil 1 minute. Remove from heat. Stir in margarine and vanilla. Pour into 4 individual serving dishes. Lay a piece of wax paper over each pudding to prevent a film from forming. Serve warm or chilled.

Yield: 4 servings

1 serving contains:

Cal	Prot	Fat	Chol	Carb	Fib	Sodium
221kc	7gm	4gm	2mg	41gm	0	176mg

Pineapple-Cherry Sherbet

John's childhood favorite.

1/4 cup egg-substitute or 1 egg equivalent

2 egg whites

1 (12-oz.) can skimmed evaporated milk

4 cups skim milk

1-3/4 cups sugar

1 (20-oz.) can crushed pineapple with juice

1/2 cup whole maraschino cherries

1 teaspoon vanilla extract

Fresh mint sprigs

In a large bowl, beat egg-substitute and egg whites with a whisk. Add evaporated milk, skim milk, sugar, pineapple, cherries and vanilla. Stir to blend well. Pour into two (2-quart) shallow casseroles. Cover with foil or plastic wrap and place in freezer until frozen. Let stand at room temperature 5 minutes before serving. Spoon into dessert dishes. Garnish with mint.

Yield: 19 servings

1 serving contains:

Cal	Prot	Fat	Chol	Carb	Fib	Sodium
127kc	4gm	trace	2mg	28gm	1gm	59mg

Spiced Peaches

Make an extra batch to have on hand.
Try pears for a change.

1/2 cup sugar

1 cup water

1 cinnamon stick

3 whole cloves

4 peaches, peeled, cut in half

Whipped Topping, page 304

In a large saucepan, combine sugar, water, cinnamon and cloves. Add peach halves. Simmer until tender. Do not stir. Chill before serving. Top with Whipped Topping, if desired.

Yield: 4 servings

1 serving without topping contains:

Cal	Prot	Fat	Chol	Carb	Fib	Sodium
128kc	1gm	trace	0	34gm	2gm	1mg

Apple Crepes

A simple, impressive dessert.

**5 cooking apples, peeled, sliced,
about 5 cups**

1/2 cup sugar

1/4 teaspoon ground cinnamon

6 Dessert Crepes, page 84

1/2 recipe Orange Sauce, page 240

2 tablespoons powdered sugar

Cook apples in a medium-size sauce-pan over medium heat until soft. Stir in sugar and cinnamon; set aside, keep-ing warm. To serve, spoon about 3 tablespoons cooked apples into center of each crepe; fold over one side then the other. Spoon 1 table-spoon Orange Sauce over each crepe. Sift a dusting of powdered sugar over each crepe and serve.

Yield: 6 servings

1 serving contains:

Cal	Prot	Fat	Chol	Carb	Fib	Sodium
224kc	3gm	1gm	trace	52gm	3gm	63mg

Whipped Topping

Wonderfully versatile dessert topping.

1 envelope unflavored gelatin

5 teaspoons water

1/3 cup boiling water

1 cup non-fat powdered milk

1 cup ice water

3 tablespoons sugar

3 pkgs. artificial sweetener

1/3 cup oil of choice

1 tablespoon lemon juice

1-1/2 teaspoons vanilla extract

Chill mixing bowl and beaters for at least 1 hour. In a small bowl, combine gelatin and 5 teaspoons water; let stand 2 to 3 minutes to soften. Add boiling water and stir to dissolve; set aside to cool. Pour powdered milk into chilled bowl. Add ice water, stir well, then beat on high speed until it holds a soft peak. In a small cup, combine sugar and artificial sweetener. Gradually add to whipped mixture, scrape sides of bowl and continue beating. In a small cup, combine oil, lemon juice and vanilla. Add to whipped mixture, then slowly add gelatin. Continue beating about 1 minute until thickened, scraping sides of bowl often. Spoon into a freezer container. Cover and place in freezer until ready to serve. Remove from freezer a few minutes before serving.

Yield: 24 (1/4-cup) servings

1 serving contains:

Cal	Prot	Fat	Chol	Carb	Fib	Sodium
44kc	1gm	3gm	1mg	3gm	trace	16mg

Strawberry Crepes

Colorful for lunch or brunch.

**1 quart fresh strawberries,
   washed, hulled**

1/2 cup sugar

1 cup low-fat cottage cheese

2 tablespoons plain low-fat yogurt

2 pkgs. artificial sweetener

8 Dessert Crepes, page 84

**1/4 recipe Strawberry Sauce,
   page 242**

1 tablespoon powdered sugar

Set aside 8 whole strawberries. Slice remaining strawberries into a medium-size bowl. Sprinkle with sugar; set aside. Combine cottage cheese, yogurt, 1/2 cup strawberries and artificial sweetener in a blender. Process until smooth; set aside. To serve, spoon about 2 tablespoons strawberry slices in center of each crepe. Top with 1 tablespoon cottage-cheese mixture. Fold sides of crepe over filling. Pour 1 tablespoon Strawberry Sauce over crepe. Place 1 teaspoon cottage-cheese filling on top. Dust with powdered sugar. Garnish with 1 whole strawberry on each crepe. Serve immediately.

Yield: 8 servings

1 serving contains:

Cal	Prot	Fat	Chol	Carb	Fib	Sodium
160kc	7gm	1gm	2mg	33gm	2gm	158mg

Piña Colada Crepes

Pineapple and coconut makes a tropical delight.

1 (8-oz.) plain low-fat yogurt

1 package artificial sweetener

1/2 teaspoon coconut flavoring

1/8 teaspoon ground allspice

1 kiwi fruit, peeled, sliced

1 (8-oz.) can crushed pineapple, drained

1 (11-oz.) can mandarin orange slices, drained

8 Dessert Crepes, page 84

1 tablespoon powdered sugar

1 kiwi fruit, peeled, cut in 8 slices

In a small bowl, combine yogurt, sweetener, coconut flavoring and allspice. Cover and chill at least 30 minutes. In a medium-size bowl, combine kiwi, pineapple and orange slices. Add yogurt mixture, stirring gently to blend. To serve, spoon fruit and yogurt down center of each crepe. Fold sides over. Dust with powdered sugar and garnish with sliced kiwi.

Yield: 8 servings

1 serving contains:

Cal	Prot	Fat	Chol	Carb	Fib	Sodium
95kc	4gm	1gm	2mg	18gm	2gm	62mg

Variation

Substitute papaya for mandarin oranges. Use a wedge of papaya with kiwi to garnish.

Index

A

Almond-Fruit Dip 32
Angie's Baked Chicken 131
Ann's Green Beans with
  Orange Sauce 195
Appetizers 25-46
Apples
  Apples & Cranberries 285
  Applesauce Bars 261
  Betty's Apple Cookies 276
  Crepes 303
  Dutch Apple Cake 260
  French Toast with Steamed
    Apples 85
  Sewing-circle Favorite 266
  Waldorf Salad 115
Apricots
  Chicken Breast with Apricots &
    Prunes 126
Asparagus Salad 99
Audrey's Oriental Chicken 151

B

Baked Fish & Herbs 164
Baked Fish with Tomatoes 165
Baked Pears & Raisins 290
Baked Scallops with Tarragon
  177
Baking Mix 65
Bananas
  Banana Cake 262
  Banana-Raisin Bread 71
Basic Crepe Batter 84
Basic White Sauce 236
Bean Enchiladas 182
Beans
  Bean Enchiladas 182
  Chicken Chili 147
  Clara's Sweet-Tart Vegetable
    Salad 114
  Enchilada-Bean Bake 185
  Garbanzo-Bean Spread 28
  Hints for Preparing Dried Beans
    48
  Lentil Soup 59

Minestrone 60
Refried Beans 203
Refried-Bean Dip 29
Slow-baked Beans 202
Spanish Lima Beans 197
Special Occasion Three-bean
  Salad 92
Spicy Garbanzo Beans 43
Beets
  Orangy Beets 106
  Pickled Beets & Onions 109
Bell Peppers
  Stuffed Peppers 158
  Vegetarian Stuffed Peppers 191
Best Oatmeal Cookies 273
Betty's Apple Cookies 276
Biscuits
  Cheesy 66
  Herb 66
  Home 66
Black-eyed-Pea Soup 51
Blueberries
  Blueberry & Peach Crisp 286
  Blueberry Muffins 67
  Blueberry Tea Cake 263
Bran 12
  Oat-Bran Muffins 68
Breads 63-85
Brenda's Breaded Fish 166
Broccoli
  Chicken & Broccoli Casserole
    134
  Joyce's Cream of Broccoli Soup
    58
  Tuna Divan 179
Broiled Turkey Cutlets 124
Brown Rice 215
Brown-Rice Pilaf 200
Brown-Sugar Cookie Icing 284

C

Cabbage
  Coleslaw 94
  Frozen-Cabbage Salad 101
  Red Cabbage 204
  Salad 100
Cakes
  Banana Cake 262
  Blueberry Tea 263

Caroline's Chocolate 264
Dutch Apple Cake 260
Gingerbread 268
Johnny's Oatmeal 265
Peach Torte 289
Pineapple-Cherry Upside-
  Down 269
Sewing-circle Favorite 266
Strawberry Shortcake 267
White 270
California Chicken Salad 93
Candied Acorn Squash 198
Cantaloupe Bowls 259
Caper Sauce 232
Caroline's Chocolate Cake 264
Carolyn's Cauliflower Salad 102
Carrots
  Carrots & Squash 206
  Gingered Carrots 205
  Glazed Carrots & Zucchini 207
Cathy's Baked Chicken 129
Cauliflower
  Carolyn's Cauliflower Salad 102
  Zippy Cauliflower 208
Celery Sauce 236
Cheese Sauce 230
Cheesey Chicken Sandwich 250
Cherries
  Cherry Cobbler 287
  Chilled Cherry Soup 50
  Pineapple-Cherry Sherbet 301
  Pineapple-Cherry Upside-
    Down Cake 269
Chicken
  Angie's Baked Chicken 131
  Audrey's Oriental Chicken 151
  California Chicken Salad 93
  Cathy's Baked Chicken 129
  Cheesey Chicken Sandwich 250
  Chicken & Broccoli Casserole
    134
  Chicken & Sweet Potatoes 135
  Chicken & Vegetable Casserole
    136
  Chicken au Gratin Casserole 137
  Chicken Breast with Apricots &
    Prunes 126
  Chicken Breasts with Cling
    Peaches 125
  Chicken Chili 147
  Chicken Dinner in a Pot 153